The Intimate and The Ultimate

Vinoba Bhave was born in 1895 at Gagode, a village in the Indian state of Maharashtra. The son of Brahmin parents, he took a vow of lifelong celibacy and service to others at the age of ten. The turning-point in his life came in 1916 when he met Mahatma Gandhi, joining his Ashram at Ahmedabad and becoming an ardent follower of his principles of nonviolent social change. He is best remembered for founding the Bhoodan or land-gift movement in 1951, and his subsequent walking mission throughout India urging wealthy landlords to give land to the poor. At the age of seventy-five Vinoba, described as the most notable spiritual figure in India after the death of Gandhi, took a vow of silence and spent the last years of his life in prayer and contemplation. He died in 1982.

The Intimate and
The Ultimate

Vinoba Bhave

Edited by Satish Kumar

Element Books

© Brahma Vidya Mandir 1986
First published in Great Britain 1986 by
Element Books Ltd
Longmead, Shaftesbury, Dorset

Set in 10½ on 13pt Linotron Palatino
by Characters, Taunton, Somerset
Printed in Great Britain by Billings
Hylton Road, Worcester

Designed by Humphrey Stone

British Library Cataloguing in Publication Data
Bhave, Vinoba
The intimate and the ultimate.
1. India — Social conditions
I. Title II. Kumar, Satish
954   HN683
ISBN 0-906540-89-5

Contents

Introduction

The name of Vinoba Bhave has resonated throughout India since the death of Mahatma Gandhi. His name summarises the qualities which made the great master. Vinu is another name for Ganesh, the elephant-headed god of wisdom. Ba, meaning Mother, was added to his name later because of his motherly and feminine qualities. Bhave denoted his Brahmin background.

As Mahatma Gandhi introduced nonviolence to the struggle for India's political independence, Vinoba Bhave used the technique of compassion to bring about social and economic reforms. For eighteen years he walked all the nooks and corners of that vast subcontinent. Every village, every town, every hill, every river, every valley he passed through vibrated with his love and laughter.

His mission was to establish a kingdom of compassion and to abolish oppression. His method was to stay in touch with Mother Earth and so he walked on his two legs. His feet reached parts of India no other mode of transport could have reached.

Vinoba's movement was to make it possible for every man and woman to share the fruits and bounty of Mother Earth. What kind of family is that in which only some children get the loving care of their mother and others are deprived, questioned Vinoba. The answer was obvious. Working on the land, with the soil, among plants, around trees and beside animals uplifts us physically, materially, economically and spiritually. Why on earth do only a few people own the land and the rest have no share in it?

1

Land belongs to God, it belongs to all or to none. Nobody created the land, then why should anyone claim to possess it? Air, water, sunshine, forests, hills, rivers and the earth are part of our planetary heritage. No one group or individual has a right to own it, possess it, spoil it, pollute it or destroy it. We can receive the earth's fruits as God's gift and return what we do not need to God. And so Vinoba knocked at every door, persuading landlords, capitalists and communists to establish a new relationship with the earth and its people. He won the hearts and minds of many millions. People relinquished some of their attachment to property and shared it with the poor and the peasantry. Vinoba collected five million acres of land in gifts to be distributed among the people. If you are rich, give; if you are poor, give. No one is a 'have not'. Some possess land, others property and yet others intellect and physical labour. Furthermore love and affection permeate the hearts of all human beings. We all have something to give, so give and give.

Through the campaign of giving gifts Vinoba inspired people to make a gift of land, gift of labour, gift of money, gift of tools, gift of knowledge. This was economics of the imagination. Hardly anybody refused this divine beggar. Vinoba's practice was never to antagonise the landlords, but to assist them to act rightly. The spirit of giving cannot be developed in an atmosphere of opposition and confrontation. Opposition reduces the chances of a change of heart and is itself a form of violence. Instead of creating an atmosphere of sympathetic understanding, it creates insecurity through which a man is drawn to defend himself just at the point when he should be taking a new impartial look.

He continued: "Take the example of a house. You want to enter the house, but it has high walls around it. You go to the wall and fight to get past it. You cannot. What happens? Your head is broken. But if you find a small door, you can get into the house and go wherever you want. But you have to find the door. Like that when I meet a landlord he has many faults and shortcomings, and his egotism is like a wall. But he has a little door, a little goodness in his heart. When you are prepared to find the door, you rise above your own egotism and you enter his life. Don't worry about his faults, find the door. I am in search of that little door in every capitalist and landlord. If sometimes I cannot find the door it is my fault, my fault that I am banging my head against his shortcomings."

Vinoba himself was without personal ambition. For him life was a search for knowledge of God. He saw the problems of India not as political or economic problems, but as spiritual problems. He had immense faith, he believed that if the landlords were not converted today, they would be converted tomorrow.

Vinoba was a saint, scholar, sage and servant of God all rolled into one. Because of these qualities Mahatma Gandhi chose him to be the first *Satyagrahi* (truthful campaigner) to end British Rule. Introducing Vinoba to the people of India the Mahatma wrote:

"Who is Vinoba Bhave and why has he been selected for offering individual civil disobedience? He is an undergraduate, having left college after my return to India in 1916. He is a Sanskrit scholar. He joined the Ashram almost at its inception. He was among the first members . . . In order to better qualify himself, he took one year's leave to further his studies in Sanskrit. And practically at the same hour at which he left the Ashram a year before he returned to it without notice. He has taken part in every menial activity of the Ashram from cleaning the streets to cooking. Though he has a marvellous memory and is a student by nature, he has devoted the largest part of his time to spinning in which he has specialised as very few have. He believes in universal spinning being the central activity which will remove poverty from the villages of India. Being a born teacher, he has been of the utmost assistance in the development of education through craft. Vinoba has produced a textbook, taking spinning as the example. He has made scoffers realise that spinning is the craft *par excellence.* For perfect spinning, probably, he has no rival in all India. He has totally rejected the idea of untouchability. He believes in communal unity with the same passion that I do. In order to know the best mind of Islam, he gave one year to the study of the Koran in the original. He, therefore, learned Arabic. He has an army of disciples and workers, who would rise to any sacrifice at his bidding. He is responsible for training a young man who has dedicated himself to the service of lepers. Though an utter stranger to medicine this worker has by singular devotion mastered the method of treatment of lepers and is running several clinics for their care. Hundreds owe their cure to his labours. Vinoba believes in the necessity of the political independence of India. But he believes that real independence is impossible without a constructive programme. He believes that the spinning-wheel is the most suitable symbol of nonviolence. He has never been in the limelight on the political platform. With many co-workers he believes that silent constructive work with civil disobedience in the background is far more effective than the already over-crowded political platform. And he thoroughly believes that non-violent resistance is impossible without belief in and practice on constructive work."

But this was not the first time that Gandhi had talked or written about Vinoba. In June 1916, he had informed Vinoba's father: "Your son is with me. He has acquired at so tender an age such high-spiritedness and asceticism as took me years of patient labour to do." To Vinoba Gandhi wrote: "I don't know what epithet to use in respect of you. Your love and character overwhelm me." Another time, Gandhi described Vinoba's qualities thus: "He is one of the few pearls in the Ashram. They do not come like others to be blessed by the Ashram, but to bless it, not to receive but to give!"

In 1932 Vinoba wrote a letter to Mahatma Gandhi giving the details of his work in the villages and seeking his guidance. In his reply, Gandhi wrote: "If something must be said, it is enough to say that the fiery ordeal you are going through would build a bridge between heaven and earth!" Some time later, Gandhi again wrote to Vinoba: "Your love and faith fill my eyes with tears of joy. I may or may not deserve them. But they are sure to do you infinite good. You will be an instrument of great service."

The Mahatma proved absolutely right. When Gandhi was assassinated in 1948 Vinoba was seen as a natural successor to his heritage. People looked to him to continue Gandhi's work of spiritual and social upliftment through pure means and simple living.

Vinoba plunged into a new experiment of liberation from the money-economy. He started working in the fields for hours on end, digging the stony ground with the pick-axe and making the land fit for cultivation. He and his co-workers took a solemn pledge to eat only what they could grow on the Ashram land and to wear only what was spun and woven by themselves. All donations except in the form of labour were strictly ruled out. Vinoba started digging a well. Hundreds of volunteers and students from places nearby participated in this project and after the day's work assembled for community prayers at sunset. Vinoba, with his body besmeared with earth, used to conduct the prayers standing. While singing in a loud voice the devotional songs, he virtually danced with joy and exhilaration.

Living without money and on gifts was something Vinoba prescribed to many voluntary workers and social activists. When I went on my peace walk around the world Vinoba advised me to go without money. He said: "Money makes a man arrogant. After a day's walk of twenty miles you will be exhausted, tired, hungry. You will find a restaurant to eat in and a hotel in which to sleep. The next day you will be on your feet again. You will not need people. But if you have no money you will be forced to find a kind, hospitable person to give you bed and bread. You will need to learn to be humble and accept all people as they are, not choose, not judge, not discriminate. With money, you think you can buy what you want and

5

therefore you can choose whom you wish to meet and whom you wish to avoid. For voluntary promoters of peace among all people such likes and dislikes cannot be an asset. Be free of the money-economy. Go to work for peace with love in your heart, trust in people and faith in God." I followed his advice and was grateful for it.

Vinoba learned his first lessons of faith, gift and spirituality from his mother, Rukmini, who was a devout Hindu. She knew hundreds of religious and devotional songs by heart and sang them much of the time. One day a beggar came to Rukmini's house to ask for alms. Rukmini gave him a generous amount of rice. Vinoba was a bit puzzled and asked his mother: "Aren't you encouraging idleness? The fellow seems to be young and strong. Why shouldn't he work for his keep?" Vinoba's mother was not impressed by this rational questioning. She replied: "Who are we to distinguish between the deserving and the non-deserving!" Rukmini always asked Vinoba to shed fear of any kind, be generous to all beings and serve others at all times. The seed of deep spirituality nurtured and nourished by Rukmini grew strong and by the age of eleven Vinoba made a vow of life celibacy so that he could devote himself to self-realisation and service to people. His two brothers also took a vow of celibacy at an early age.

Vinoba never enjoyed school and longed to get out of it. He used to remark to his friends that the existing schools and colleges were only large factories for training 'your most obedient servants'. One day while he was sitting beside his mother in the kitchen, Vinoba took out a roll of papers in his hands and offered it to the fire. "What are you doing?" asked his mother in astonishment. "I am burning my school and college certificates."

"But you may need them some day."

"No," said Vinoba emphatically. "They will be of no use to me hereafter." All the certificates were soon consumed.

Vinoba told his companions that he was thinking of giving up his college studies. A couple of days before the examinations were due to be held in Bombay, Vinoba boarded a Bombay-bound train with a friend. He got off half-way and handed a letter to his friend with instructions not to post it until the examinations were over. The letter was to his father: "I am sure you have trust in me wherever I may go, I will not indulge in unethical behaviour."

Vinoba went to the holy city of Benares, the great centre of Sanskrit languages and spiritual learning. Sitting by the banks of the Ganges, he studied, contemplated, meditated and philosophised with sadhus and scholars. Finally, Vinoba felt that these holy men were cut off from the real world. In the dualism of God and the world the meaning of wholeness was lost. God can only be realised through the world. It was then that Vinoba discovered Mahatma Gandhi; Gandhi who was struggling to free India from the clutches of the British Raj, who was campaigning to liberate the untouchables from the shackles of caste domination, who was working to revitalise rural life, and who was living in a community which worked through prayer and purification. Vinoba went to Mahatma Gandhi's Ashram and both felt a deep attraction for each other. At last Vinoba had found his mentor and master. From then on Vinoba devoted his life to seeking God and serving the people, particularly dedicating himself to the poor of India.

Vinoba's desire to serve the poor found its form in the village of Pochampalli where the untouchables were beginning to rise against the landlords. Vinoba walked there to see for himself what was happening. The harijans (untouchables) surrounded him and begged him to help them. They explained that they were unemployed and had no land. If they only had land they could support themselves. Vinoba did not know what to do. He asked all the harijan families to get together and come to a public meeting in the evening. All forty families of landless labourers, poor and hungry, as well as landlords, attended the meeting. After prayers and spinning one of the harijans stood up and spoke passionately. "We shall serve Mother Earth and receive her fruits, the only solu-

7

tion for our poverty is land. Please give us land." Vinoba asked how much land they needed. They discussed among themselves and said: "We are forty families, two acres per family will be quite adequate, altogether we need eighty acres." Vinoba had no answer. Quietly he said he would ask for land from the government. And, then it suddenly struck him that someone in the village audience might like to donate some land for these poor harijans. He lifted his eyes, gently smiled at the gathering, and without expecting any response remarked rather casually: "Brothers, is there anybody amongst you who can help these harijan friends? They are prepared to work hard on the land to earn their livelihood." And one of the local landowners, Ramchandra Reddy, stood up, looked at Vinoba and said: "My father had willed that out of two hundred acres one half should be given away to some deserving persons. All these years I did not know what to do. But today is a golden opportunity for me. Please accept my donation of one hundred acres. I shall be most grateful for this act of grace."

Neither Vinoba nor the members of his party could believe these words; they appeared to be too good to be true. But Ramchandra Reddy continued standing and awaiting Vinoba's response. Vinoba was overwhelmed. It was a miracle. The harijans had asked for only eighty acres, and the donor had spontaneously offered a hundred. Vinoba looked once again towards the harijans. Although they had heard of the offer of a hundred acres, they kept to their original figure of eighty acres. They repeated their assurance that they would serve Mother Earth with all their heart. There was not the slightest trace of greed or temptation. After wiping his tears, Vinoba remarked: "I came here with empty hands and will go to the next village tomorrow morning again with empty hands. Both the donor and the donee are present here in our midst. Let them exchange the land in our presence. The donor should also help the harijan friends with some money and implements for cultivating the land in a co-operative way."

8

Ramchandra Reddy gently bowed before Vinoba and accepted the responsibility. The harijans also touched his feet with joy and satisfaction. Vinoba appointed a committee of five on the spot, consisting of the donor, two representatives of the harijans and two experienced farmers of the village. Vinoba declared: "Man does not act merely on the strength of his own thinking. There is always a Divine hand behind such noble actions. I am a man of faith, and work in the name of God. If Providence desires to take work from me, I will walk from village to village to seek land donations for the poor!" This was the birth of the great Land Gift Movement.

Living like the poor, loving the poor and seeing God in the poor does not mean accepting the domination and exploitation of the poor. Vinoba became a fearless defender of the poor. So many poor have nothing to live on because some of us have too much. We don't know when enough is enough and therefore we have a bottomless bog of greed. Vinoba asked people not to pity the poor but to live like the poor. By pushing the poor into the trap of misery and starvation we are only hurting ourselves. The poor are members of our human family, they are part of us. If you have five sons consider the poor the sixth son and share the sixth part of your possessions with the dispossessed.

This kind of conviction carried such a power that successive prime ministers and presidents came to see Vinoba in the thatched huts or bamboo cottages where he camped during his long walks through the country. Vinoba always avoided capital cities. Where the poor were not welcome, Vinoba would not go, whether it was a palace or a temple. It was a mark of Indian spirituality that a man like Vinoba could command such respect from politicians and ordinary people alike.

At the age of seventy-five Vinoba decided to relinquish all action. He entered the fourth stage of life.* He stopped his travels, took a vow of silence and spent his time in prayer, meditation and contemplation.

At the age of eighty-seven he felt weak and unwell. He saw

the Death God slowly approaching him. Doctors tried to protect him from the final departure, but Vinoba had no fear of death. If life was a celebration, death was the culmination of it. Vinoba stepped forward to embrace death. He renounced all food, drink and medicine. When he undertook this magnificent fast all his friends and followers knew that the great departure was imminent. In their thousands they gathered near Vinoba from all over India. After eight days Vinoba made his journey to the heavens in total peace.

SATISH KUMAR
HARTLAND, 1986

* According to the Hindu way a human life has four stages. The first stage is preparation and learning without being absorbed into the nitty-gritty of life. Stage two is experiencing and carrying out the responsibilities of a householder, being a host, a bearer of children, a winner of bread and dispenser of wordly affairs. Stage three is passing the family and business responsibilities to the children and pursuing the service of the needy, upliftment of the poor, realisation of the arts, music and poetry and undertaking pilgrimages. The final stage is renouncing it all, surrendering to God, working at self-realisation and preparing for the next life. Vinoba bypassed the second stage but he followed the rest meticulously.

1

Education or Manipulation

Barbarous state

The importance of formal education has been exaggerated beyond all reason, and as a result our methods of education have become ridiculously unnatural and harmful. If a child appears to have a quick and retentive memory, he is pushed excessively to learn. His parents and teachers wonder how much can be rammed into his head. If the child is slow he is often deliberately neglected. Clever pupils manage somehow until they reach college, but then many of them fall behind. If they do not lose ground in college, they frequently fail to achieve anything worthwhile in after life. This is because their immature minds have been loaded with too heavy a burden. When a horse is lively and runs well there is no need to whip it along. You can see that it is a good runner, so why not leave it alone? When you use the whip, what happens? The horse shies and falls into a ditch, and brings down the rider with it. This kind of pressure is barbarous, and should be done away with as a method of education.

As soon as the pupil begins to feel: "Now I am learning", something is wrong with the educational machinery. The best form of physical training and development of the body for little children is play. While he is playing the outside world does not exist for him. Children at play are absorbed in one undivided experience. They are not aware of comfort or discomfort, they feel neither hunger nor thirst, neither pain nor weariness. For them play is a joy, not duty; it is pleasure, not physical training. This principle has to be applied to all kinds of learning. Instead of the artificial idea that education is a duty,

11

we must foster the natural and inspiring idea that education is a joy. The feeling among schoolchildren is that education is punishment. As soon as the restless energies of the child begin to develop, as soon as there is a tendency to independence, the family decide that it is time for him to be shut up in a school. The meaning of school is – a place for shutting children up! Teachers who set their hands to this work are merely school jailers.

The teacher should be free from the professional attitude, "now I am teaching my pupils". Unless the guru himself is a single-minded, natural teacher, the pupils cannot learn naturally. Whenever you find yourself saying that "we are teaching by the Froebel, or Pestalozzi, or Montessori method", you may be sure that this is empty verbiage, the meaningless copy of some method or other; it is a ghost, it has no life. Education is not like algebra; it is not a matter of applying the formula and getting the answer ready made. Education is a well-spring within, overflowing naturally into the outer world. Even though this natural education may have its faults, it is workable. What must never be tolerated is the orderly doling out of ignorance by slaves who follow a fixed method, which is nothing but systematised ignorance. Herbert Spencer, the educational philosopher, has commented that "education has no power to fashion an outstanding personality". What value then can be attached to educational techniques? These systems must be able to make the promise that, by knowing this you will grow wise and your work will be fulfilled. Any educational technique that cannot give this undertaking is simply an organised effort to throw dust in the eyes of ordinary people. Did Shakespeare study any theory of drama? Has anyone been made a great poet by learning by heart the rules of rhetoric? There is no great meaning or value in the words 'system' and 'method' in themselves. They are a delusion.

Those seers who were gifted with the deepest insight made it abundantly clear that they did not know how education is given. As is said in the *Kena Upanishad*, "He knows who says:

'I do not know'." Method, syllabus, timetable – these are all meaningless words. They are nothing but self-deception. Education is to be had only from living deeds. When some separate activity, unconnected with the work of life, is given the name of education, this 'education' has a poisonous and unhealthy influence on the mind, just as some foreign substance entering the body usually has evil consequences. Unless we are exercised in work we have no hunger for learning, and when learning is forced artificially upon a man who has no appetite for it, the digestive organs have no power to digest it. If wisdom were to be had by cramming books, the library cupboards would be wise indeed. But learning which is forcibly crammed in is not digested. Mental dysentery sets in and the intellectual powers are atrophied and die. Let us therefore define education as 'that which, without method, builds itself up into a methodical and ordered whole, that which no teacher can give and which nevertheless is given'.

The true teacher does not teach, yet one may educate oneself at his side. The sun itself *gives* its light to no one, yet all, in the most natural and easy way, receive its light.

Anything which is cut off from life loses its power to teach. The attempt to divide education from life and its problems is like putting off the thought of death. In reality we are dying every moment and the day of death is only the final stroke. He is truly free who 'dies before his death', by facing the fact of death with open eyes. He who accepts the steady approach of death as part of experience will find death gentle. He who tries to escape from that experience, to tear it out of life, will find death sits like a nightmare on his shoulders. The blind man knows that there is a pillar in his path only when he strikes his head against it; the man who sees it ahead of him avoids the crash.

Teaching must take place in the context of real life. Set the children to work in the fields, and when a problem arises there give them whatever knowledge of cosmogony, or physics, or any other science, is needed to solve it. Set them to cook a meal, and as need arises teach them chemistry. In one word, let them live. The children should have someone with them, but that someone should not belong to a special category called teacher, he should be a man living an ordinary life in the practical world. The man who is to guide children should conduct his life intelligently and be capable of explaining the processes of life and work to the children as opportunity arises. It is not education to fill students' heads with information, but to arouse their thirst for knowledge. Teacher and pupil both learn by their contact with each other. Both are students. True education is that which is experienced, tasted and digested. What can be counted and recorded is not education. Education cannot be doled out; it cannot be weighed and measured.

In the *Upanishads*, the praises of ignorance are sung side by side with the praises of knowledge. Man needs not only knowledge but ignorance too. Knowledge alone, or ignorance alone, leads him into darkness. But the union of fitting knowledge with fitting ignorance is the nectar of eternity. The world is so filled with the matter of knowledge that men would go mad if they were to attempt to cram all of it into their heads. The ability to forget is just as necessary to us as the ability to remember.

Self-reliance

Many people would agree about the importance of self-reliance in education. Self-reliance has a very profound meaning. There must be economic self-reliance through manual labour. Everyone must learn how to use his hands. If the whole population were to take up some kind of handicraft, it would bring all sorts of benefits; class divisions would be overcome, production would rise, prosperity and health would improve. So that, at the very least, this measure of self-sufficiency must form part of our educational programme.

Education must be of such a quality that it will train students in intellectual self-reliance and make them independent thinkers. If this were to become the chief aim of learning, the whole process of learning would be transformed. The present school syllabus contains a multiplicity of languages and subjects, and the student feels that in every one of these he needs the teacher's help for years together. But a student should be so taught that he is capable of going forward and acquiring knowledge for himself. There is an infinite sum of knowledge in the world, and each one needs some finite portion of it for the conduct of his affairs. But it is a mistake to think that this life-knowledge can be had in any school. Life-knowledge can only be had from life. The task of the school is to awaken in its pupils the wish to learn from life.

Most parents are anxious for their children to complete the school course so that they can get a salaried job and lead an easy life. This is the wrong way to look at education. Learning has value in its own right. The purpose of learning is freedom. Freedom implies not only independence of other people but also independence of one's own moods and impulses. The man who is a slave to his senses and cannot keep his impulses under control is neither free nor self-sufficient.

The question "What shall we teach our students?" is raised in the *Upanishads*, and the answer given is that we should teach them 'the *Veda* of *Vedas*'. We teach the *Vedas*, but omit the Bible; we teach the *Bible*, but omit the *Quran*; we teach the *Quran*, but omit the *Dhammapada*; we teach the *Dhammapada*, but omit science; we teach science but omit political economy. Where are we to stop? No, we have to give them instead the *Veda* of *Vedas*, that is to say, the key to study the *Vedas*, and everything else for themselves. We have to put into their hands the key to knowledge.

The things we set children to learn are bound to be forgotten; they are not worth remembering in full. And because we know this, we allow them to pass if they get thirty-three per cent of the marks. A boy who gets thirty-three percent of the marks is sixty-seven per cent a failure, but we have to pass him. It is of no use for him to remember them, and so we give him so much margin. On the completion of his education a student ought to have confidence in his own powers. This is what matters, not a supply of miscellaneous information and a degree.

The goal of education must be freedom from fear. In the *Upanishads*, when the guru is teaching his disciples he says to them: "O my students, whatever good conduct you find in me, that follow; whatever you do not find to be good, that do not follow." That is to say, the guru gives students freedom. He tells them to use their own judgement in deciding what is right and what is wrong. They are not to think that whatever their guru says is wholly right. It is certainly true that the guru is endeavouring to live by the truth, otherwise he would not be a guru; but he nevertheless cannot claim that his every action will be in harmony with truth. And so he tells his students to be alert, to use their intelligence and examine his conduct, and to disregard whatever seems to them wrong. And by this means he enables his students to grow in fearlessness.

Fearlessness means that we should neither fear anything, nor inflict fear on others. Both those things are parts of fearlessness. A tiger cannot be called fearless; it may not be afraid of any other animal, but it is afraid of a gun, and it also inspires fear in other creatures. True fearlessness neither enslaves another, nor does it slavishly submit to another.

The only sufficient basis for such fearlessness is the knowledge of the self. This self-knowledge is the foundation of education. But the education which children get today is the direct opposite of this. If a child commits some fault we slap it, and it begins to obey us because it is afraid. But we have taught it nothing of truth by our action. Until education is really based on fearlessness there is no hope of any change in society. We ought to teach children never to submit to those who beat and strike them. The pity is that even fathers and mothers do it. God has given them a child who trusts their every word, who has complete confidence in them. God has put into the parents' hands such a completely trustful disciple, and yet he gets beaten. We have to begin the teaching of fearlessness in the family and continue it in the school.

No knowledge without action

The fountainhead of all the world's conflicts is that knowledge has been separated from action. They have been separated intellectually by faulty psychology; they have been separated in life by faulty sociology; and they have been assigned diffe-rent market values by faulty economics. There is no such thing as knowledge divorced from action. There is only one excep-tion to this rule, and that is the knowledge that 'I am, I exist'; the knowledge of the Self *is* divorced from action. It is beyond action. But all other knowledge is linked with action. There is no knowledge without action and no action without know-ledge. The two are one, this is not a question of technique, but is a fundamental principle of Basic Education. People ask, "If children have to work for two or three hours every day, how are they to learn anything?" It seems to me an extraordinary question. What we should really be asking is how they are ever going to learn anything if they spend three or four hours a day poring over books. It is amazing to think what three or four hours of reading really means. In three hours a boy might read sixty or seventy pages of a book but does he really *learn* anything? The muscles of his eyes no doubt get some exercise. We never seem to have any doubt that by reading he is obtain-ing knowledge, and that reading is in fact the direct road to knowledge. It is nothing of the sort; on the contrary, book-learning is like a curtain that shuts us off from the real world.

There is a book called *The ABC of Bee-keeping*, in which every possible piece of information about bee-keeping is to be found. Having read it I thought: "Now we can do something; let us get hold of some bees." But I did not get them without many days of running around, and when I had got them, it took two full months more to win their confidence. Everything was written in the book and the book was certainly of some help, but the main road to knowledge is direct action. Reading and study are supplementary to action, they are tools. It is like saying "That man has no spectacles, how can he see?" The

17

eyes, not the spectacles, are the organ of sight; if the eyes are weak, spectacles can certainly assist them.

The separation of learning from labour results also in social injustice. Some people do nothing but study and others nothing but hard labour, and as a result society is split in two. Those who earn their bread by manual labour form one social class and those who do only intellectual work form another. In India, manual labourers are paid one rupee a day, intellectual workers are paid twenty-five or thirty rupees. A very great injustice has been done by rating the value of manual and intellectual work so differently. And it is the abolition of such injustice that must be the goal of our education.

Even if these differences are done away with, that is not enough. The more closely we can live in harmony with Nature, the greater our welfare and happiness will be; the more we are cut off from Nature, the less contented we shall be. The smallest possible percentage of our population should be employed in agriculture, and the largest possible percentage in other productive kinds of work. But at the same time the life of the whole population should be closely in touch with agriculture. If a single person is cut off from the life of the land, his life will lack completeness. Everyone needs to be in touch with the land, to be rooted in the soil. Human lives are like trees, which cannot live if they are cut off from the soil, but at the same time the business of agriculture must be done so efficiently that the smallest possible number of people are tied entirely to the land. These two principles may seem to be mutually contradictory, but they are both parts of Basic Education. It is a basic need of humanity to be in touch with the earth, and any nation or civilisation which is cut off from it slowly but surely loses its vigour and degenerates.

Basic Education is bound up with Nature; how can any such education be carried on in our large cities? It is a great misfortune for the cities to be cut off from the earth, for human life could suffer no greater loss. When I was in gaol everyone got the impression that I was enjoying myself. One day the gaoler said to me: "You seem to be very content; is there nothing that you miss?" "Yes," I said, "there is one thing." "What can it be?" he asked. "Why don't you guess?" I said. "I will give you a week to do it." He thought it over for a week and then he said, "I don't know what it is that you miss." I told him. "I am very content with everything else, but I am sad that I can never see the sunrise and sunset."

How much joy there is in being able to go out in the open air, among the natural objects of creation! City-dwellers cannot know this joy, so what do they do, poor things? They get a flowerpot and put paper flowers in it, and hang pictures of sunrise and sunset on the walls. So artificial has their life become, that at night they cannot see the stars. How can our cities be blessed with the sight of the starry heavens, in the midst of all their artificial lighting? What is left, I sometimes wonder, for these people to burn? They have burned up even the darkness, the darkness of night, which was given to man for peace, rest, and quiet thought. This means that the task before education is to change the whole system of values and way of life that is current in our cities. No joy is to be compared with this joy of the free life. There is a word in Sanskrit for this boundless joy, the word *sukha*, well-being and contentment. In Sanskrit the primary meaning of *sukha* is 'the wide and boundless sky'. Happiness is to be found beneath the open sky. It is hard to find it where life is artificial and the sky is cramped.

If a man's house is full of medicine bottles, we infer that the man is probably ill. But if his house is full of books, we conclude that he is intelligent. Surely that is not right? The first rule of health is to take medicine only when it is absolutely necessary. By the same token, the first rule of intelligence ought to be to avoid, so far as possible, burying one's eyes in books. We consider medicine bottles to be the sign of a sick body; we ought to consider books, whether secular or religious, as the sign of a sick mind!

The wise men of past ages, the fragrance of whose lives still

19

fills the world, took no pains to make life literate, but to make it meaningful. We do not need to look far in our modern educated society for illustrations of the truth that a literate life may be meaningless. History on the other hand is full of examples of how meaningful an unlettered life may be. Indeed, when we compare the lettered with the unlettered, the 'a-lettered' as we might say, it often seems that this letter 'a', the sign of deprivation, is really the sign of honour. Does not Krishna say in the *Gita*: "Among the letters of the alphabet, I am A"? We should not attach excessive importance to literacy as such.

Books, after all, contain only letters, and it is vain to hope to make life meaningful merely by collecting books. Whose stomach is filled by talking of curry and rice? The well in the book drowns none, the boat in the book saves none. The dictionary says that 'steed' means 'horse', and we think that we can find the meaning of 'steed' in the dictionary. But that is not so. The meaning of the word 'steed' is not to be found in the dictionary, it is standing in the stable. It cannot be got into a dictionary. What the dictionary tells us is merely that the word 'steed' and the word 'horse' have the same meaning. What that meaning is you will find in the stable. The meaning is not in the book. Until we understand this, we shall never taste true knowledge.

God put into man's mind the powers of intellect, and hunger into his stomach, and universal sympathy into his heart. Man was thus equipped with three tools of knowledge, a sympathetic heart, a questioning intellect and a hungry stomach. In order to appease his hunger he has to use to the full his gifts of co-operation and intelligence. As soon as he sets to work, he begins to acquire knowledge of many kinds.

Student-teacher comradeship

An interesting light is cast on the Indian attitude to education by the fact that in all fourteen languages of India there is no root word corresponding to English 'teach'. We can learn, we can help others to learn, but we cannot 'teach'. The use of the two distinct words, 'teach' and 'learn', suggests that these two processes may be thought of as independent of one another. But that is merely the professional vanity of the 'teacher', and we shall not understand the nature of education unless we rid ourselves of that vanity. Our first task is to realise that an 'uneducated' human being is nowhere to be found. But today, all too often, an ordinary schoolboy treats a first-class carpenter as if he were an ignorant boor. The carpenter may be a man of maturity and experience, a wise and skilled workman, who is of real service to his community. But simply because he cannot read and write, the 'educated' boy treats him as an inferior.

The gift of education is not a matter for pride, in fact an essential condition for being able to receive it is that we should grow in humility. In our ancient books *vidya* (education) is equated with *vinaya* (humility); *vinaya*, in Sanskrit, is a synonym for education, and a student who had completed his studies was called *vinit* – perfected in humility. This humility is the fruit of true education. The teacher must be ready at all times to serve his students in humility; the students must learn humbly from the teacher. Teacher and student must each regard the other as a fellow worker. In former times they united in the ancient prayer of the schools: 'May the study of both of us be filled with vigour '. The teacher does not consider himself to be 'teaching', but to be studying. The prayer asserts that both study together. They both understand that the teacher finds his own true good in helping the student, and the student in helping the teacher.

Wherever two people live together in this kind of comradeship, giving and receiving mutual help, there real education is in progress. The place of books is, therefore, secondary. This idea troubles many people, who think that if the place assigned to books is reduced the students will be deprived of the most valuable tools of knowledge. Books do have a place as tools of knowledge, but it is a very minor place. The major need is for teacher and student to become work-partners, and this can happen only when the distinction between the teacher 'teaching' and the student 'learning' can be overcome.

In matters of knowledge no orders can be given. Education does not 'discipline' students, it gives them complete freedom. Whether or not a society free from governments is ever built in the larger world, such a society must be found in the world of students. If there is one thing of supreme importance for students, it is this freedom.

In such conditions we may certainly expect the students to imbibe the spirit of self-government. Our present social framework *is* artificial, it is based on class-consciousness. Educated boys ought to be rebels against its values. We should oppose existing society, oppose it with humility, but oppose it with conviction. Such humility is the antithesis of slavish submission; it is a strong humility that is able to stand up against the wrong values of society.

Many people think of 'Basic Education' as a new kind of system, method or technique of teaching. This is a mistaken view. I am very much afraid of systems, especially in educational work; a system can make an end of all education. What a student receives from a *Nai Talim* (Basic Education) centre is not a system to be practised but a compass to show the direction. *Nai Talim* is a suggestion which we may keep in our mind but we must make our own independent judgements and try out our own independent experiments. *Nai Talim* is not a system, it is an idea, a seed-thought.

It is a fault in the western system of education that it lays so little stress on learning by heart. The exalted experiences which are recorded in our literature should be stored in our minds. Indian traditions in this matter differ from those of the west. The point of view of western scholars is analytical; they break up the world into fragments and divide it into various 'branches' for study; but we look upon the world as one, and study it as an integral whole. And for this reason there is in our tradition a place for the learning of great passages of literature by heart. Western traditions give the foremost place to the intellect. The importance of the intellect is recognised by all, but one must not ignore the feelings and emotions. The heart of man needs nourishment no less than the mind.

The school-society must be a model of the future society. Let us suppose there are five to ten teachers, with ten to twenty other members of their families. There are sixty to eighty children – altogether a hundred people or so. They should have tools to work with, land to grow crops, whatever books they need and other equipment provided by society. Then say to them: "Earn your living and carry on your education at the same time."

All this no doubt seems difficult. It seems difficult because we all come from a class to which ideas like these are new. But what a small class it really is! Society as a whole is a society of workers, and in the end our teachers must come from this working society. We shall not have a good educational system until we can train workers as teachers. Knowledge means direct action, direct experience. That kind of learning we do not possess. We have no real experience. And therefore our learning does not give us vigour and strength.

Education is like the water in a river – what is here today is not what was here yesterday, and what is here today will not be here tomorrow. The river goes on flowing but its water is never the same. In the same way education should go on changing continually, with the experience of every passing day.

Each region is different, and plans for education must take account of those differences. Education will take one form in a town on a river bank, another in a town on a hill, another in a town near a forest. It must vary with the circumstances. The same fixed mould, the same set of textbooks, will not be equally suitable everywhere. When there is just one textbook for the whole State no attention can be paid to these local features and variations; in consequence the student's interest is not awakened, and the special needs of the individual town are not met. Teaching ought to fit the situation.

We eat today to satisfy today's hunger; we do not eat for ten days ahead; similarly the student should be given the knowledge that is needed to satisfy the demands of his life today.

If we reckon our syllabus by subjects – geography, history, arithmetic, geometry, and so forth – there will be no end to it, and no value. Instead let us think in terms of the development of speech and of reason, the development of the body, the mind, and the senses. We should not think in terms of subjects or books, but of people. Our task is to nourish them, their reason, their intelligence and so on. Our aim is not to develop the individual's technical skill, nor is it to turn out educated workmen. What we are aiming at is the full and total development of human potentiality. If they get 'mere knowledge' or 'mere manual skill', or even both, their education will be one-sided. For manual skill and knowledge are only two out of very many aspects of human capacity, and what we look for from education is the development of the whole.

Disgusting examinations

Examinations seem to me to provide a most disgusting picture of the old educational system. When we take an examination, a supervisor has to be appointed to watch us, to see that no student steals from another by copying. It is to me a very saddening spectacle. For if it is possible to suspect us of being capable of stealing, then, as students, we have already failed. What is there left to examine?

I have no real knowledge of the subjects in which I have had to take examinations, but I do know well things in which I have never been examined. My own experience, therefore, does not lead me to attach any value to examinations. Examinations are exactly like the purgatives that people take to cleanse the stomach – one takes an examination and all one's knowledge is cleared out! There is no reason why we should fall into this trap which the pedagogues have set for us.

If I want to teach children about doors and windows I will ask them what windows are for. Then, when they have seen clearly why we need windows and doors, I will say: "Now tell me, what windows and doors have you got in your own bodies?" Eyes, ears, mouth, nose, etc. are called 'doors' in Sanskrit. I will then ask the children to draw a window, an eye – there comes practice in drawing. After that I will tell them about various kinds of windows that people have made – there is history. Can these old windows be seen anywhere in the world today? I will take them to Lapland and in that connection tell them about the life of the people there. In short, one should tell children about the way of life of different countries in connection with some such natural interest.

China like India is an ancient country with a wealth of population and intensively cultivated. Why is China so productive? What do they do to maintain the fertility of the soil? In this connection I will tell the children about manures. We have to learn from China in particular how to make use of human excreta. This is very widely used in China and thanks to it the soil maintains its productivity even though it has been farmed for so many years.

An American has written a book called *Farmers of Forty Centuries*, describing the agriculture of China. In it he says: "How thriftless we Americans are! We possess fifteen or twenty acres of land a head, and we have farmed it for only four centuries at most. Yet we use all kinds of chemical fertilizers to make it productive, and these ruin the soil, while we allow a valuable manure like human excreta to go to waste."

If it rains very heavily the children should be given a holiday and enjoy themselves playing in the rain. The teacher too should take his clothes off and play with them. We in India get a holiday when it rains, but in England they should get a holiday when the sun shines. Why? Because there the sky is usually dull and overcast, so there when the sun comes out is a holiday. In this way, while they are playing and enjoying themselves, I can give them some idea of the climate of England.

But, this kind of extensive knowledge should never be given

apart from a natural context of interest. It will not do for the teacher simply to get up and talk about Lapland; let the natural opportunity arise. It is the teacher's task to seize the natural opportunity to widen the children's knowledge.

Lies of history

One of the faults of our education is what goes on in the name of history. The lies of history are much more serious than those of fairy-tales; the story-teller does at least begin by avowing that his story is fiction. The historian, on the other hand, is apt to claim for his fabrications the sole title to truth! Does anyone imagine that what is taught in the name of history is the truth? There have been two world wars in this century; one version of their 'history' is written in Germany, quite another version in Russia, still others in America and England. I was amused to read in the newspapers that Russian history is to be corrected and rewritten – what was glorious in Stalin's time has now apparently become false! In Stalin's time Mahatma Gandhi was described as a counter-revolutionary; now he may become a great man. Perhaps we should thank God that they never went so far as to claim that he never existed! But 'history' is dictated by the whims of those in power; they use the events of the past as tools to distort men's minds. And this is the 'history' that is taught to students. The makers of history are dead and gone, but our brains are burdened with their deeds. What use is there in knowing what happened in the past and gabbling lists of dead kings? Countless kings have come and gone in the world, thick as leaves on a tree. Why study their history? The fact is that in the name of history the thinking of people is being forced into particular moulds, and the result is prejudice.

Are we to make new history, or merely to read old history? We should not smother the creative spirit under the passive study of history, and infer that "there is nothing new under the sun". Why should people say that what has never yet happened can therefore never happen? Why should we be born at all, if we are only to do what has been done already? We must not allow our intellects to be crushed under the weight of ancient history. We have been born to make new experiments and to test new truths. We must free ourselves from this load of history.

Take a topical example. Every state seems to be trying to extend its boundaries into the territory of other states – and 'history' is responsible for it. Everyone has his vanity fed by reading the old histories that were written to glorify his own country. Pakistan and India, through their newspapers, accuse each other of violence and unprovoked attacks. Where is the authority that can judge between them? Until the greed and nationalism encouraged by history is destroyed, there can be no peace.

The guru is God for his disciple, and the disciple is God for his guru. The knowledge which the disciples get from their guru should be full and complete, the service which they render to their guru should also be full and complete. The guru should find the nurture and teaching of the students a wholly satisfying task for its own sake, it should not appear to him to be a means to any other end. It is extremely valuable that teacher and students should work together in some kind of productive labour such as growing food, making cloth, cleaning etc. and that they should live as a commune. They should feel that their study is also part of their contribution to society. If this is the pattern of labour and study, there will be no problem of suitable books; the necessary books will be made on the spot as the fruit of these two kinds of common experience.

The best books we possess in India have been based on this kind of practical teaching experience. Whenever a teacher and student study and act together, the fruits of their experience are not confined to their own place, but are available for the whole world to profit from.

What we expect from centres of Basic Education is that ideas shall be thoroughly studied and canvassed and also tried out in practice. The teacher and the students will together plan, discuss and conduct experiments to test out their theories, and as a result of their work the world will be enriched with knowledge united with experience. Where a vigorous churning of ideas is integrated with practical experimental actions, there we have Basic Education. Where there is merely the discussion of ideas without a practical basis, we have the old type of education which is so common everywhere. Where there is practical work and experience, but no thinking or discussion, we have the bodily labour which is being carried on by innumerable peasants and workers. The Basic Education teacher and student must unite in their own persons the peasant with the philosopher.

In this connection we may take Krishna as our example, for he did not merely repeat the philosophy of his predecessors, he developed it. Before his time the paths of knowledge, action, meditation and devotion were already known. Krishna blended these various traditions into an integral whole.

'Only teaching'

A young man said that he wished to do some good work for society. "Tell me," I said, "what kind of work do you feel you could do well?"

"Only teaching, I think," replied the young man, "I can't do anything else, I can only teach, but I am interested in it and I feel sure I shall be able to do it well."

"Yes, yes, I do not doubt that, but what are you going to teach? Spinning? Carding? Weaving? Could you teach any of these?"

"No, I can't teach those."

"Then tailoring, or dyeing or carpentry?"

"No, I know nothing about them."

"Perhaps you could teach cooking, grinding and other household skills?"

"No, I have never done any work like that. I can only teach ..."

"My dear friend, you answer 'No' to every question, and yet

28

you keep saying you can only teach. What do you mean? Can you teach gardening?"

The would-be teacher said, rather angrily, "Why do you ask all this? I told you at the beginning, I can do nothing else. I can teach literature."

"Good! Good! I'm beginning to understand now. You mean you can teach people to write books like Tagore and Shakespeare?"

This made the young man so angry that he began to splutter. "Take it easy," I laughed. "Can you teach patience?" That was too much. "I know what you mean," I said, "You can teach reading, writing, history and geography. Well, they are not entirely useless, there are times in life when they are needed. But they are not basic to life. Would you be willing to learn weaving?"

"I don't want to learn anything new now. Besides I couldn't learn to weave, I have never before done any kind of handwork."

"In that case it might of course take you longer to learn, but why should you be unable to learn it?"

"I don't think I could ever learn it. But even supposing I could, it would mean a lot of hard work and a great deal of trouble. So please understand that I could not undertake it."

This conversation is quite enough to enable us to understand the psychology and characteristics of far too many of our 'teachers'. To be 'only a teacher' means to be:

completely ignorant of any kind of practical skill which
    might be useful in real life;

incapable of learning anything new and indifferent towards
    any kind of craftsmanship;

conceited;

and buried in books.

'Only teaching' means being a corpse cut off from life.

Living dead

Some people call this living corpse an 'intellectual worker'. But this is a corruption of language. In the *Gita* it is said that those who are slaves of the senses, who are burdened by attachment, are not the bearers of wisdom. The life of adulterous intellect is death, and those who live it are the 'living dead'. The existence of those who live by 'only teaching' is a living death.

In former times a teacher used to be called *'acharya'*. An *acharya* is one who is perfect in right living and who does not sell himself for money.

Teachers should give up the mistaken notion of 'only teaching' and take upon themselves the responsibility for their own living, just as the workers and peasants do. They must let their pupils share fully in this responsibility and make their whole environment a means of education: that is, they must let the education come about of itself. ''The *Vedas* should be read after the earning of a livelihood has been completed.'' We ought to spend the greater part of the day in working for our living, and regard all this as essentially educational work; in addition we should set aside an hour or two specially for new learning.

It is important to make our own lives a pattern of what the life of society ought to be. If a man can really fulfil his own life, the radiance of education will stream out of itself upon everyone around him, and the atmosphere of the whole neighbourhood will feel its influence. A teacher like this is a school in himself, and to live with him is real education.

The teacher in the school should be the inspiration of the whole town, and the school should be the centre of service. If the community needs medicine, it should be supplied through the school. If the streets need cleaning, the school should initiate the work. The people should turn to the teacher to help them settle disputes. The school should make plans for the observance of festivals. In this way the school should become the centre of the community; it should develop whatever is of value and introduce the things that are lacking.

The most important thing for the students is to preserve the independence of their minds. If anyone has a right to full freedom, it is the student. Knowledge cannot be had without trust, but it is equally essential that the student should have intellectual freedom. Many people think that trust and intelligence are incompatible, but that is a mistake. The ear and the eye are different senses, but they do not contradict one another, and it is the same with trust and intelligence. Without trust it is impossible to learn anything. The mother points to the moon and says: "Look, my little one, that is the moon." If the child had no faith in his mother, if he were to say to himself: "Who knows whether what she shows me is really the moon or not?" he would learn nothing. So that trust, or faith, is fundamental to learning. Knowledge begins in faith, but it is perfected, completed, in independent thought. Students, therefore, must never let go their right to freedom of thought. A teacher who tries to compel the students' assent is no teacher. We must not allow our independence of thought to be interfered with, and we must guard the privilege of freedom.

I want to warn students that their right is in danger of being lost in the modern world. An attempt is being made, in the name of 'discipline', to force all students' minds into the same mould. In the name of discipline we are imposing mechanical uniformity, and this causes injury to students' minds.

Government control of education is dangerous

Throughout the world education is under the control of governments. This is extremely dangerous. Governments ought to have no authority over education. The work of education should be in the hands of men of wisdom, but governments have got it in their grasp; every student in the country has to study whatever book is prescribed by the education department. If the government is fascist, students will be taught fascism; if it is communist, it will preach communism; if it is capitalist, it will proclaim the greatness of capitalism; if it believes in planning, the students will be taught all about planning. We in India used to hold to the principle that education should be completely free from state control. Kings exercised no authority over the gurus. The king had absolutely no power to control education. The consequence was that Sanskrit literature achieved a degree of freedom of thought such as can be seen nowhere else, so much so that no less than six mutually incompatible philosophies have arisen within the Hindu philosophy. This vigour is due to the freedom of education from state control.

The status of teachers has sunk so low that they feel themselves to have no authority at all. They must follow whatever path the government directs. They are under orders, the servants of authority. They may perhaps modify the government schemes by a comma here or a semi-colon there, but they cannot do more than that. Today there is an attempt to expand education and the number of schools and of teachers is being increased, but the spirit of the true guru is not there. A good teacher means one who is a good servant; a bad teacher means a bad servant; good or bad, he remains a servant.

All this results from the fact that the education department is a government department, it is not independent. The judges of the high court are also appointed by the government, and they are bound by the laws which the government makes. Nevertheless, they are much more independent. They have the power, within the bounds of law, to give a verdict against the government. The teacher ought to have a much greater freedom than the judge, yet today the education department is less independent than the department of justice.

The universities should demonstrate how every student, by his own labour, can gain food through knowledge and knowledge through food, nourishing his stomach with his two hands and his mind with his two eyes. They should show how the breach between knowledge and work can be closed. The students should have no fees to pay, there should be no hostel expenses and no salaries for the teachers. The workshop, the library and the laboratory should be provided by the government. There should be no need for holiday periods, for no one will feel any sense of confinement there.

The universities of today are not fitted for the poor, even though a few poor students may be admitted without fees as an act of grace. But the universities we envisage should be open to all. If the children of the rich cannot adjust themselves to such hard work, we may have to excuse them from an hour or two of labour as an act of grace.

At present even agricultural colleges are located in towns, and no student is admitted to them unless he has passed certain examinations. This means in fact that a boy is admitted to the agricultural college only when it is certain that he will be quite unable to work in the fields in the cold and dew, the sun and rain. The professor and students learn agriculture while seated at ease in their chairs! For experimental purposes, there is an apology for a field, and even that is in the charge of labourers – it is they who carry out the experiments.

Even in higher education students should work six hours a day to earn their bread and should be taught, in two hours a day, all the knowledge and science which relates to their work. There should be no cost either to the school or to the parents, and rich and poor should be treated alike. There should be a university in every village. People now think that every village ought to have a primary school, every big village or town a high school, and a big city a college. But if the creator had made such a plan, the villages would be peopled by children of under ten years, the big villages and little towns by young people of fifteen or so, and cities by older people. But when all the business of life from birth to death is transacted in villages, why should not the whole learning of life be available also in villages? Some poverty-stricken minds are planning for only one university in each state, but according to my plan there must be a university in each village. There is no meaning in giving four years of education in the village and then requiring children to go elsewhere if they want to go further. I ought to be able to get a complete education in my own village, for my village is not a fragment, it is an integral whole. My plan is for a complete and integrated village community where every aspect of life is complete.

Countless poor children all over the world have to begin working for their bread at a very tender age; and even so they do not get enough to eat, still less do they get any education. At the same time, other young people, right up to the age of twenty-five, are getting a travesty of education; they give their minds to finding ways of getting rich without working, while millions of people who do work cannot even get enough to eat. Our motto must therefore be: "Education for self-sufficiency up to sixteen, education through self-sufficiency after sixteen." Unless we make our educational plans on this basis, those twin evils of our present system will not be overcome.

Our forefathers had made provisions to enable villagers to have access to kinds of knowledge which no one in the village possessed. This plan must be carried on. It is the tradition of the wandering *sannyasi* (holy man). The *sannyasi* travels continually among the villages for the greater part of the year, remaining in one place only for the four months of the rainy season. The villagers thus get the full benefit of his knowledge. He can teach them both knowledge of the world and knowledge of the Self. A *sannyasi* is a walking university, a wandering school, who goes at his pleasure to each village in turn. He will himself seek out his students, and he will give his teaching freely. The villagers will give him fresh, wholesome food, and he will need nothing else. They will learn from him whatever they can. There is nothing more tragic than that knowledge should be paid for in money. A man who possesses knowledge hungers and thirsts to pass it on to others and see them enjoy it. The child at the breast finds satisfaction, but the mother too takes pleasure in giving suck. What would become of the world if mothers began demanding fees for feeding their babies?

Bought knowledge

The 'knowledge' which is purchased for money is no knowledge at all; knowledge bought for cash is ignorance. True knowledge can only be had for love and service, it cannot be bought for money. So when a wise man, travelling from place to place, arrives at a village, let the people lovingly invite him to remain a few days, treat him with reverence and receive from him whatever knowledge he has to give. This is quite a feasible plan. Just as a river flows of itself from village to village, serving the people; just as cows graze in the fields and return of themselves with full udders to give the children milk; so will wise men travel of themselves from place to place. We must re-establish this institution of the wandering teacher. In this way every village can have its university, and all the knowledge of the world can find its way into the villages. We must also reinvigorate the tradition of the *vanaprasthashram* (a state of freedom from worldly responsibility) so that every village gets a permanent teacher for whom no great expenditure will be incurred. Every home must be a school, and every field a laboratory. Every *vanaprastha* must be a teacher and every wandering *sannyasi* a university. The students are the children and young people who want to learn; in every village there will be people who give an hour or two to learning and spend the rest of the day working. This seems to me to provide a complete outline of education from birth to death.

The purpose of this education is that the village as a whole shall solve the problems of its life by its own strength. The wealth and resources of the village must therefore belong not to individuals but to the village itself. Only then is it possible to plan for all children to have an equal chance of education. If we cannot even give them all their share of pure and nourishing food, how can we give them an equal education?

Sudama was the son of a poor Brahmin; Krishna was a prince, a king's son. Both lived in their guru's home, ate the same food, shared the same labour, were given the same knowledge. How can there be real school in a village when one comes in rags and another in fine clothes, when one boy comes to school fasting and another has stuffed himself until he is lethargic? If we desire that everyone should have a proper education, we must arrange that the villagers live like one commune, and all the wealth, all the wisdom, all the strength of the community should be used for the good of all.

If you ask someone what he is drinking he will answer 'tea'. There is sugar in it, but he never mentions the sugar, he never says he is drinking tea-and-sugar. The sweetness of the sugar permeates the tea, but the man drinks and says nothing about it. Education must be like the sugar, doing its work in secret. We can see the hands, nose, ears, eyes and tongue are active, but no one can see what the soul is doing. Our ears appear to be listening, our tongue appears to be talking. No matter what the appearance may be, it is not *only* the tongue that talks. In spite of appearances, it is not only the ears that hear. That which speaks and hears is the spirit within. And the spirit is invisible. The best education is similarly invisible. The more it is seen, the more imperfect it is.

2

People's Power

Freedom from government

'*Sarvodaya*' means freedom from government; it implies decentralisation of power. We want to do away with government by politicians and replace it by a government of the people, based on love, compassion and equality, where decisions are taken, not by a majority, but by unanimous consent; and they are carried out by the united strength of ordinary people. Then only will we be able to establish *Sarvodaya* – 'the upliftment of all'. This is possible only by means of nonviolence.

In India we have the Asoka's emblem of four lions. It is a symbol of nonviolence. Cows and sheep herd together because they are cowards; there is no courage in a flock of sheep (sheep are not nonviolent, merely timid). The lion has courage, he is lord of the jungle, but the mark of his lordship is a vast consumption of his subjects! The lion is bold, but violent, and because he is violent he is solitary. Asoka, however, brought together four lions and thus created a new type of lion – brave, but bound by ties of affection to others. Sheep stick together but have no courage; lions have courage but no love. When courage and love are found together, there we have nonviolence. The strength of nonviolence lies in this union. We want people to have the courage of the lion, but we do not want to live separated like lions but to live in unity. That is real revolution.

The strongest institutions in the world today are of two types; religious, and governmental. At the time they were formed, society recognised them to be essential and found them useful. But as things are today it is necessary that society should be set free from both these types of institution. I do not mean that we need to get rid of religion; what we need is to get rid of religious institutions. I do not mean, either, that there should be no orderly provision for the public welfare, but we need to get rid of institutions which exercise authority in the name of service.

In India the institution of monarchy existed from very ancient times but the kings were chosen by the people and they ruled with the help of the *rishis,* the sage-philosophers. They used to go to the *rishi* whenever any important question arose. In practice therefore it was the *rishi* who ruled; but he ruled from his *ashram,* he did not occupy the throne. The king would hasten, time after time, to seek out the *rishi,* and the *rishi* would ponder the king's problems and give a considered reply. The king would then abide by what he said. These *rishis* were not elected. They remained in their *ashrams,* engaged in meditation and gave thought to the welfare of the world. They practised self-restraint, and in their solitude undertook fasting and other austerities, living on herbs and roots, and striving to subdue lust and anger. Such were the *rishis* whose word was law with kings in affairs of state.

There is a passage in the *Upanishads* where a king declares that in his kingdom there is no thief and no miser. Where there are misers there are thieves, for the miser is the father of the thief. It is the miser who is responsible for the increase of theft. And no one in his kingdom was ignorant. There was no one who did not know how to read and write. There was also no one who did not worship God. Here in India the tradition of learning and self-knowledge dates from very ancient times.

Today we live in an age of expanding science, an age also which inherits the traditions of a thousand years of wisdom. We ought to be able to see that in such times it is right and proper for every man to take charge of his own affairs, both in matters of knowledge and in matters of religion. It is quite wrong that a few people should be able to confer favours, and that the rest should be burdened by those favours. The good work which is done by government services is very far from good in its effect upon the minds of the people. When the elections take place, the government party asks for your votes because of all the good work they have done. It is true that they have done good work, the people will be oppressed by the sheer weight of their charity – and that is exactly what saddens me. Some people ask why I do not protest strongly when the government does something wrong. It is true that I do not make such protests, though I may raise the subject if occasion offers. But I do raise my voice when the government does something good. There is no need for me to protest against the government's faults; it is against its good deeds that my protests are needed. I have to tell the people what sheep they are. Is it a matter for rejoicing if you all turn into sheep and tell me how well the shepherds look after you? It seems to me that it would be better if the shepherds neglected their duty – you might then come to your senses and remember that you are after all not sheep but men – men capable of managing your own affairs.

That is why my voice is raised in opposition to good government. Bad government has been condemned by everyone. People know very well that bad government should not be allowed, and everywhere they protest against it. But what seems to me to be wrong is that we should allow ourselves to be governed at all, even by a good government.

There is a saying in Sanskrit, "After royal power comes hell." The *rishis* say in the *Vedas*: "Let us strive for self-government". "I do not want government, I want self-government." What is managed from the capital is government, even though it is that of our own people. What goes on in a local area, where every man manages his own life, is real self-government. When I decide that I will not steal, even though I am hungry, that is self-government. If I am under some other person's command, where is my self-government? Self-government means ruling your own self. To that end we must build up

39

popular strength so that people have a sense of their own power. We must find the courage to believe that we are capable of managing the affairs of our own community. It is one mark of self-government not to allow any outside power in the world to exercise control over oneself. And the second mark of self-government is not to exercise power over any other. No submission and no exploitation! This cannot be brought into being by government decree, but only by a revolution in the people's way of thinking.

I am continually urging that believers in nonviolence should use their strength to establish *lok-niti* – government by the people: in other words to put an end to *raj-niti* – government by politicians. We want not a kingdom ruled by political 'kings', but a commonwealth ordered by the 'common' people.

There is a false notion in the world that governments are our saviours and that without them we should be lost. People imagine that they cannot do without a government. I can understand that people cannot do without agriculture, or industries; that they cannot get on without love and religion. But governments do not come into these categories.

I once suggested that all our administrators should be given leave for two years, just to see what would happen in their absence! Would any of the ordinary work of the world come to an end? Would the dairyman no longer make butter or the market gardener sell vegetables? Would people stop getting married and having babies? If the sun failed to rise, the world would indeed end; if the rains of divine grace were to cease, the world would end. What we really need is divine grace, not official grace, and if the government were to take leave for two years it would destroy the popular illusion that a government is indispensable.

The best kind of government is one where it is possible to doubt whether any government exists at all. We ourselves should be seeing to the affairs of our own community instead of handing over all power to the centre. And central authority ought to model itself upon the divine government – unseen, unfelt, decentralised. How many hours a day does God have to work to run the world? Hindus will tell you that He does not work at all. The government is not an activity, it is a thought. The less the activity, the better the government. An ideal government would have no armaments, no police force and no penalties; the people would manage their own affairs, listen readily to advice, and allow themselves to be guided by moral considerations.

Thought is at the basis of human life. Thought is responsible for change and progress. Ideas start movements, build up strength and create new life. Then the social structure changes, the pattern of life changes. The French Revolution was brought about by an idea. Marx wrote, and nations were shaped by his thought. Man is strong because of his thought. He eats and drinks, but with it and behind it all there is an idea.

The principle of *Sarvodaya* is that the good of all is contained in the good of each. It is impossible for the real interests of any one person to clash with those of others. There is no opposition between the real interests of any one community, class or country. The very idea of conflicting interests is a mistaken one; one man's interest is another's, and there can be no clash. But if we look upon evil as our good, and consider that our welfare consists in what is really injurious, then our 'interests' will come into conflict. If I am intelligent and in good health, this fact is in your interest. If I get water when I am thirsty, it benefits not only me but you also. If we imagine that our interests conflict it is because we have a false notion of what constitutes our interest. Revolutionary ideas cannot be spread by a government. The government can only act on an idea when it has been generally accepted – and then it is compelled to act on it. If it does not, it will be replaced. In a democracy, the government is the servant and the people are the masters. When you want to get an idea accepted, do you explain it to the servant or to the master?

41

The authority of the government is incapable of bringing about any revolutionary change among the people. If such a popular revolution were attainable through governmental authority, why did Buddha give up his royal power? However, people point out that after *Asoka* was converted, he used his royal power for the propagation of religion. But I must say that the decline of the Buddhist faith in India dates from the day when it received the backing of governmental power. When the Christian faith was backed by the imperial power of Constantine it became Christian only in name. The pure religion practised by the first disciples of Christ was seen no more and hypocrisy entered the life of the church. History shows that when the religious movements won royal favour they were joined by thousands who were not real religious devotees, but merely loyal devotees of the ruling king. If there should be any genuine encounter between the state and religion, religion would destroy the power of the state. The two can no more exist together than darkness and the sun. The exercise of power over others is not in accordance with religious principles. Religion serves all, religion pleads its cause in love.

What strength is there in the government that is not also in us? It can get some things done by the use of money – but whose money does it use? It is our money, which we hand over in the form of taxes. The government is not in business on its own account, it possesses only what we give it. We may be poor, but our government is even poorer than we are, for all that it has is only a fraction of our wealth. We are the well and the government is the bucket. The wealth produced by the combined labour of people is a great deal more than the amount we let the government have. The government appears to be wealthy only because what it has is concentrated. Our own wealth is not so conspicuous because it is dispersed among our many homes.

The Five Year Plan of the Indian government envisages an expenditure of eight hundred million rupees a month. This works out at about two rupees a month for four hundred million people. That is what the great government plan boils down to. A child can earn two rupees in one day by spinning, so that even a child can produce more than the government plan. Well, what is the government going to do with those two rupees? There will be railways, schools, agriculture and commerce. Factories will be opened, scientific research will be undertaken, literature will be encouraged and languages taught. All this will come out of those two rupees. If the people were to rely on themselves, they could do more than that. How is wealth produced? By labour. Who does the labour? The people. So that any power of the purse wielded by the government can never be a match for that wielded by the people.

There remains the power of the law. Do you imagine that the reason why there are so few thefts is that there is a government law against theft? That society is shaped by edicts and by punishment? Society does not derive its ethical traditions and its general high standards of conduct from legal enactments, but from the teachings of the good and wise who have given mankind its scriptures. No one ever reads the government's laws. The social wealth of the nation consists in the general goodness of heart which prevails. But government has no power to lead men to righteousness; it has no power to inspire men to noble deeds. The people themselves have more power than the government to spur men to action. Is it right, then, for us to think that the government ought to do everything? If we lose our own energy and initiative and expect the government to do everything for us, our society will not prosper. Let this society of ours do something to help itself. Progress will come when every individual is prepared to act for the sake of the community. In *Sarvodaya*, each person is encouraged to be upstanding and self-reliant.

The ultimate goal of *Sarvodaya* is freedom from government. I use the words freedom from government, and not absence of government. Absence of government can be seen in a number

43

of societies, where no order is maintained, and where anti-social elements do as they please. That kind of absence of government is not our ideal. Absence of government must be replaced by good government, and afterwards, good government must be replaced by freedom from government. A society free from government does not mean a society without order. It means an orderly society, but one in which administrative authority rests at the grass roots. For this reason, we must rouse the people to an awareness of their own strength, that they may stand on their own feet.

Theories of government

Let us look at three different theories of government. The first is that the state will ultimately wither away and be transformed into a stateless system; but, in order to bring that about, the state must at present exercise maximum power. Those who accept this theory are totalitarians in the first stage and anarchists in the final stage.

The second theory is that some form of government has always existed in the past, exists now, and will continue to exist in the future; a society without a government is a sheer impossibility. Therefore society must be so ordered as to ensure the welfare of all. There may be a certain amount of decentralisation, but all important matters must be under the central government. The supporters of this theory hold that government must always exist, and that a government elected by society must have an overall control of affairs.

The third theory, which is ours, is that in the preliminary stages a certain measure of government is necessary but it will become progressively less necessary. There should be no totalitarian dictatorship to ensure progress towards a stateless society. We propose to proceed by decentralising administration and authority. In the final stage there would be no coercion but a purely moral authority. The establishment of such a self-directing society calls for a network of self-sufficient units.

Production, distribution, defence, education – everything should be localised. We shall thus achieve decentralisation through regional self-sufficiency.

The need for organisation in the economic sense will gradually diminish and ultimately disappear altogether. The centralisation of the whole, or the greater part, of the government system makes its subsequent dissolution more difficult. Therefore decentralisation must be introduced at once. It is not necessary that every village should immediately produce all its needs. The unit for self-sufficiency may be a group of villages. All planning must be directed towards a progressive abolition of government control by means of regional self-reliance.

Every individual should become as self-reliant as possible. That is God's plan, after all. He has not only given each man feeling and intelligence and other inner qualities, He has also given each a number of external organs: eyes, ears, nose, etc. He has not made us specialists, giving one ten eyes and another ten ears or hands; we do not need to run to one another for help in order to see or hear. God has gone in for such thorough decentralisation that He need exercise no control. But our centralised arrangements will never bring us nearer to a stateless society. So long as one place specialises in sugar, a second in food-grains and a third in oil, there will always be the worry of arranging for transport and distribution; and if disputes arise, some people are going to get only sugar, while others get only oil.

We hold elections and send our representatives up to Parliament, and consider that we have done our job, and that the government will see to whatever services need to be provided.

The people are divided among a number of political parties and even within one party there arise sub-parties and 'group politics'. I am not suggesting that it is impossible to give disinterested service from within the government – some people most certainly can and do. But such people can be counted on the fingers of one hand. The rest enjoy the experience of

45

power, and so their work cannot be disinterested. The members of the other political parties who do not hold power are eager to win it, and they give all their attention to the business of discovering and proclaiming the mistakes made by the government in power.

As things are now, there seems to be very little faith in the strength of the people. The leaders of the political parties believe that results can be achieved only by coming into power, that is, they put their faith, not in the strength of the people, but in the authority of government. The people ask what is being done for them. This means that the people themselves have no faith in their own powers. That being so, independent public service is regarded as of no value. Some politicians do undertake it of course, but only as a means to power.

In India there are six million government 'servants', and the number is increasing. It is said to be a method of curing unemployment. But it really means that the rest of the population has got to support these millions of officials; it works out that every thirteen families have to support one family, for not only the official, but his family also becomes dependent on others. We thus create a bureaucratic 'middle class' which takes no part in productive work, and at the same time has a high standard of living. Not only are these people excused from any productive or physical labour, they also possess, if they are so minded, the power to oppress others. Moreover people are clamouring for still more jobs to be provided for the 'educated unemployed'. There can be no more fearful danger to the country than the creation of such an unproductive bureaucratic middle class; how is this enormous financial burden to be of benefit to our country?

The highly expensive adminstrative and other departments of government are known as 'services'. And there are services galore: civil service, medical service, educational service. The officials of the civil service are paid four-figure salaries, while their masters, the poor of the country, whom they profess to serve, have to starve. It is a tragic paradox that those who earn

46

millions are called servants, while those who produce food for the nation are regarded as self-seekers who work merely to feather their nest. What is one to say of these 'services'? If words are not to be deprived of their meaning, then this is nothing but cant and hypocrisy. The services of a scavenger, a mother, a professor, and numerous others of that type cannot be evaluated in terms of money. Therefore the rule should be: a man who wholeheartedly serves society should be entitled to a living wage. Likewise, all government servants, including the president of a country, should be given a living wage. The basis of payment to the president and government servants must be the same as that of the working class man and the scavenger. I have served society in various capacities, as professor, judge, peasant, writer, editor etc., but I have never experienced the feeling that one type of work was of a higher value than another. I derived the same satisfaction in every one of them. When anybody desires to give me more than I need I get perplexed. I cannot accept it. Why should I take more bread than I need? And I am at a loss to know why I should accept it, simply because somebody offers it! The economic, social and spiritual value of all work should be equal.

Before the independence of India, the work of the freedom movement was a religious duty, and even saints and hermits took part in it. In those days it was the road to strength. But today, after independence, the road to strength is to be found in people's service, in bridging the gulf between high and low, between master and servant; in arousing the strength of oppressed womanhood, in raising up the despised low castes. There are natural opportunities for renunciation in founding of a new social order.

We should create *loka-shakti* – the self-reliant 'power of the people'. It should be distinguished from the other two forms of power – the power of violence and the power of the state. The power of the people is the opposite of the power of violence, and though there is no such trenchant opposition between the power of the people and the power of the State, yet the two are different. There is of course an element of violence in the power of the State too, but inasmuch as this power has been entrusted to the State by the people, its character differs from that of naked violence and the two cannot be put in the same class. However, we intend to go further ahead and create conditions which will do away with the power of the State.

Some people ask me why I do not enter politics. I ask myself whether, if I did so, it would be possible for me to work as I do today, a free man, with nothing to hinder me from speaking the truth as I see it. Being in the government, every time I opened my mouth I should have to stop to think what would be the effect of my words. Will I gain or lose votes? I should no longer feel the spiritual strength which I experience now. I could no longer roar like a lion, I should be obliged to run tamely along a railway line, like a wagon chained to its engine, or an engine chained to its train!

If a man can swim a river with a stone tied round his neck it means that he is an exceptionally good swimmer. It does not mean that the stone is an aid to swimming. He swam the river in spite of the stone, not because of it. So, power is not an aid to people's service, though some great souls can keep their detachment in spite of their power and perform some service.

Supposing I were to run a school and make it really attractive, parents would certainly send their children to it rather than to the local government school. Consequently the government school would be closed, for what else could the government do if people did not send their children? It could only close its own school and think up some trick for capturing mine. I may then receive a letter from the government saying that as my school is running so well they are happy to offer me ten thousand pounds as a grant. If I accept the money, I am finished. I therefore write to the government somewhat as follows: "I am very grateful to the government for its kindness, but the work that I am doing is independent of the government, and government aid would injure it rather than help. I therefore cannot accept your offer." In this way we increase the people's real strength.

People go on complaining that the government has not done this and that. But after all what is a government? Is it more powerful than God Almighty? God gives us the rain, but rain alone does not guarantee a harvest. It might grow nothing but weeds. The peasant must work and sweat to get his crops. If God himself cannot give us the harvest, will the government be able to do it? What is wrong is the idea that we derive our strength from the strength of the government. The truth is just the opposite – the government derives its strength from ours. The world cannot be set free from the burden of governments so long as we depend on government for help in everything and invoke the government as though it were God. No real freedom exists today, and we shall not get it as long as we carry on with our 'representative democracy' and continue to do nothing while expecting our representatives to do everything. It is not merely that we are indolent, that we leave all the work to our representatives and do nothing ourselves; what is much worse is that the party rivalries create such hatred and friction that it is impossible for us to develop any strength of our own. Socialist and Communist, Brahmin and non-Brahmin, Hindu and Muslim – every sort of division is exacerbated and embittered in the name of democracy and freedom. Real freedom means freedom at grass roots.

The greatest drawback of democratic government is that we come to rely wholly on a handful of men. The people's lives are no longer in their own hands. A few individuals are given all the power and the rest hope that the government will protect them. Everything depends on what the man at the top thinks. We let ourselves be dictated to by a small élite in a top-heavy democracy and regard this as our security.

Throughout the world governments are elected but they are not controlled by the people. There is no need for us to use our own brains, for we have five hundred servants, our MPs, to do

all our work for us. It is they, however, who are the real masters. The people are masters in name only, they are nothing
but slaves in reality. Is this democracy? In America all the
power is in the hands of the President and a few of his
associates. If they should make an error of judgement they
might set the whole world on fire. It is a terrible thing that such
power should be entrusted to any 'representatives'. We have
no control over any part of our lives. There are marriage laws,
education laws, land laws, trade laws – nothing in life is safe
from the government's law making. This is a very dangerous
state of affairs and it exists throughout the world. We ought to
leave in the hands of our representatives only what is of secondary importance; the things that really matter ought to be done
by the people themselves.

It cannot be called a democracy when all power is centralised, when a few people are elected to office and everything is in their hands. Do you imagine that because you have
now the power to vote, you have in your hands the reality of
power? What actually happens in this voting? Out of any
hundred voters sixty may exercise their votes. This means that
a party which gets thirty votes may come into power, for the
remaining thirty votes may be divided among various other
parties. So that in fact thirty people can choose the government for a hundred.

Now suppose that a bill is to be introduced in Parliament.
The thirty elected representatives of the ruling party hold a
meeting, and possibly fifteen of them are opposed to the bill.
But however much they may oppose it in the privacy of their
meeting, they will vote for it in Parliament. As for the other fifteen, they make it their business to follow the lead of their
party chief or of one or two other shadow ministers. In this
way the real power is all in the hands of two or three individuals at the top.

Today, in the name of the 'welfare state', we concentrate all
power in the centre. Even if people do get a certain amount of
benefit out of it, I would still call it not 'well'-fare, but 'ill'-fare,

because it keeps power in the hands of a few. The political practice today is to try to use one's authority to force all sorts of things upon society, and no government goes to more frightening lengths in this matter than a welfare state. A welfare state appears at first to be a very attractive idea. People say: "The former government was just a police state; it thought of nothing except defence. Society did everything else for itself. Now that the old government has gone, our new government must give some thought to the welfare of society!" But this idea of a welfare state is not at all new! When Kalidas describes the kingdom of King Dilip, he describes what might well be called a welfare state. The king looked after his subjects in everything, he both protected and maintained them. He was, it was said, their real father – other fathers had merely begotten them! These lines of Kalidas simply horrify me. It is to me a frightening ideal of kingship. In a country where the people are so firmly under control, they can do nothing of their own initiative. The government plans for every part of the nation's work – social reform, agricultural improvement, clothing, education, defence, industrial policy, the encouragement of men of letters. The people are completely passive, they are a mere protectorate – in fact they are nothing but a flock of sheep.

This 'welfare state' involves giving a great deal of power to a few individuals, who will then control the whole life of the people. Plans for six hundred million people of India are to be made in Delhi. Decisions which touch every side of our daily lives are to be taken in Delhi. Delhi will decide what social reforms should be undertaken, what system of medicine we are to adopt, what language we are to use, what kind of cinema shows we are to see! If we hand over all this power to the state, the people lose their independence and self-reliance.

That is why, throughout the world today, there is no freedom, but only an illusion of freedom. There will be no freedom until every man in every community controls his own life. When every community runs its own affairs, settles its own quarrels, decides how its children shall be educated, undertakes its own defence, and manages its own markets, there will be a general renewal of self-confidence, and ordinary people everywhere will get some experience of public affairs. But today this know-how is lacking at the grass root level. The prime ministers of today are very much like kings. The difference is that a prime minister is ruler for five years only. A second difference is that the king's son succeeded to his father's throne, while the prime minister's son cannot. Otherwise the structure of government remains the same; the prime minister's authority is absolute for his five years, and what he says goes.

But five years nowadays can hold as much as fifty years did formerly. In the old days, when the king issued a decree, three or four years used to pass before it reached the more distant parts of his kingdom. If conditions changed in the meantime, he would issue a second decree before the first one had been fully enforced, and the second one too might take years to reach the villages. The king was king only in name. His decrees did not greatly affect the lives of his subjects, who in practice had great freedom. Things are very different now. Government orders reach the whole country on the very day they are issued. By means of mass media an order can be put into effect throughout the country within two hours. Consequently, whoever rules the country now can do more in five years than his predecessors did in fifty. Five years of today must be counted as equivalent to the whole lifetime of a former king.

We should not make the mistake of thinking that at the end of five years the people will be able to exercise some control. After five years things may be completely changed. Today there is a show of consulting the people, and consequently our rulers claim that whatever they do is done with the people's consent. Our former kings could not and did not make any such claim. Even police violence and military action are supposed to be done with popular support; the government says that it is ruling by the people's mandate and that it is obliged to fire or attack. In the old days the king's officers could not argue that they had popular support; it was the king who was responsible for their actions, good and bad alike, and he had to bear the blame. Now, however, it is the people who are responsible for the deeds of our modern 'kings'.

The whole arrangement in fact is sheer bogus. Not only does it fail to express the people's strength, it also does even more harm because governments can now claim to 'represent public opinion'. Formerly, the king chose his generals. Nowadays the prime minister chooses his associates and forms his cabinet, for otherwise, so they say, the cabinet would not be a team. Our modern democracy came into being as a protest against the power of kings, and for that reason it suffers from the same faults as the monarchy it displaced – the real power remains in the hands of a central bureaucracy. Can we say that we have freedom so long as the people do not feel themselves to possess any power? The only difference between the old monarchies and the elected governments of today is that formerly it was other people who loaded the burdens onto my shoulders, while now they are being placed there by my own hands. The new right I have acquired is the right to load myself, but it is still I who must carry the burden. We call Hitler a dictator, but he too claimed to have been elected, and by a very big majority. Among our former kings there were some tyrants who oppressed the people, but the effect of their tyranny was not very widespread. Things were very different then from what they are now. The government had very limited power, and it did not interfere to any great extent in ordinary life. It confined itself to keeping a small army to resist foreign invasion, and to making a few roads for the army's use. Kings who were inclined to benevolence did something to help the common people, but this was in the nature of personal generosity. They did not and could not control the common life. Nowadays, however, it is no longer possible to separate politics from life; the government has power to control the affairs of every citizen. The people have no right to take any decisions at all.

It will not do to make use of a few men's brains only and let the abilities of all the rest run to waste. Nowadays villagers get orders to build good roads and to clean up the village – in other words, to use their hands, not their brains. How can they be expected to take an interest in such work? But if they don't the government calls them lazy. The labourers are called 'hands' and those who supervise their work are called 'heads'. The community is cut in two. What is the use of telling a man to work if you first cut off his head? The hands can achieve nothing without the brain.

I am convinced that those who get themselves involved in the machinery of power politics, even for the purpose of destroying it, are bound to fail in their purpose. To destroy it you have to stay out of it. If you want to cut down a tree, it is no use climbing into its branches. Authority cannot be *given*, it has to be *taken*. Power will come into the hands of people when they make up their minds and take it.

We are apt to look upon the common folk as fools, but they are really very intelligent. The poor of India have been served by the saints, so when they hear that we call ourselves their servants, they put us to the test of saintliness. Their standard of living may be low, but their standard of thinking is high.

Decentralised power

Every village in India must be a nation in miniature, and its village government should have the same activities as the national government. The nation has a health ministry, so must the village; the nation has departments of industry, agriculture, education and justice; the village also must have them. The national government has relationships with foreign countries; the village also has to plan for its relationship with other villages.

When every village has its own government it will naturally

have a group of people skilled in public affairs, men of experience and wisdom. It should be quite reasonable that when a difficulty arises in Delhi the members of the central government should plan to visit two or three villages and see how the matter is being handled by experienced men there. We are told nowadays that there is no one at all in the village, no one even in the whole district, with any political knowledge or skill; perhaps there may be two or three such men in the whole state. How are we to run a free government with so few skilled men?

We must distribute in the villages the powers that are now concentrated in Delhi. What would have become of the world if the Creator-God had not shared out any of His intelligence among His creatures but kept it all to Himself in heaven – so that anyone who needed a bit would have had to wire to heaven for it? Nowadays our ministers seem to have to spend all their time rushing about in aeroplanes, but how much more running about God would have had to do! His own plan is very much more beautiful. He has given a measure of understanding to all. Intelligence is not stored up in a warehouse in one place. Is it possible for our ministers of state to enjoy carefree slumber? But the Lord sleeps – and no one even knows where He is! We shall have real self-government when our Delhi government is able to sleep like Him – when our prime minister slumbers in the ocean of Delhi.

If the village people want to see conditions in the villages improve they have to gird up their loins and get to work themselves. If anyone has no land, they themselves must see that he is given his share of the village land. They must set up industries. Just as the Delhi government has to consider what things the country should import and export, so the villagers themselves should decide what things they should get from outside, and what things they can sell. Nowadays, anyone can buy from outside whatever he fancies. But this should be decided after full discussion by the whole village. Supposing people need brown sugar and it is not possible to make it in the village immediately, the village may decide that it should be brought from outside for one year only. But the villagers would not go individually to buy it from the outside market; they would get it for a year through their own village shop, and meanwhile they would plant cane so as to provide for their own needs in the following year. From then on the local shop would stock only the local sugar. In this way the village should be of one heart. In a village of five hundred people there should be a thousand hands, a thousand feet, five hundred brains but only one heart. The five hundred minds will decide their affairs by mutual consultation.

Some people think that I plan only for self-reliance and not for mutual help. A man should not be a parasite upon others, but there should be interdependence. I too want interdependence. I drink milk, but I do not milk the cow – the people arrange for all my needs, and in return I give them what service I can. But there are two kinds of interdependence – that of the weak and that of the strong. An example of the first would be the interdependence of the blind man and the lame. The blind can walk but cannot see, the lame can see but cannot walk, so the lame man sits on the shoulders of the blind man and then the lame man looks ahead while the blind man walks. We do not want the whole of society to have that kind of interdependence. I want to see whole men, each with two eyes and two legs, walking together with hands joined in fellowship. I want the interdependence of the strong.

The job of the government is not to give orders to the village, but instead to keep the villages in touch with one another. In the same way the government in Delhi would have no authority over the states, but would maintain contact between them. The higher the level of government, the more extensive should this liaison work become, and the more limited would be its direct authority. The direct authority, the real power, should be exercised by the villages.

The centre should only offer advice which the villages should be free to accept or reject. In such a set-up, even if a few men were to fail to do their duty only few villages would have to suffer. When power is in few hands, the whole country suffers when something goes wrong. When we make our bread at home we may perhaps spoil it, but the rest of the village is all right. On the other hand, if anything goes wrong at the bakery, everybody's bread is ruined. It is possible today for governments to ruin everything, though the government can be replaced in the elections, but the new government finds itself obliged to carry on what the old one began and is bound by the undertakings of its predecessors. If the government of today makes a trade pact with foreign countries the government of tomorrow has to abide by it. That is why decentralisation of power is necessary.

Effective power must rest in the village community and the higher authorities should have only secondary powers. The national government would have advisory functions and may co-ordinate roads and railways, foreign relations etc. It would offer much less temptation to ambitious men to recapture power, for the real power would be in the village.

The distribution or dispersal of the functions of government is an instrument for creating strength among the people. These activities and the authority deriving from them, should not all be concentrated at one place, but should , on the contrary, be widely distributed among the villages. If we do not distribute the powers and functions of government, we shall be obliged to submit to military authority. We shall never be able to dispense with the army in the future any more than we can today. We must make up our minds once and for all to submit to an army and to keep it ready. We shall not be able to look forward to any future date when we shall be able to do away with it.

But if you do want to get rid of the army, then you must decentralise. We ought to manage our affairs of state in the manner that people would begin to wonder whether there was any authority at all.

The village *panchayats* which we once had in India were a great

57

boon. The food production of the village, its education, its defence, and all other important affairs were handled by the *panchayat*. In the *panchayat* all five castes united to manage their affairs; it was a common organisation for all. All the land belonged to the *panchayat* and a portion was given to every farmer for cultivation. In the same way the washerman, the barber etc., all had their share. Thus the whole village lived like a family and the *panchayat* managed its affairs. That was real self-government.

The Indian idea of a village *panchayat* holds a special place among the political ideas of the world. It included the principle that the five members of the *panchayat* must reach a common mind, and then only the decision was made. It was a kind of security council of the village. But now we 'pass' a decision by a majority of four to one or three to two. In my opinion only that proposal deserves to 'pass' which recommends itself to all. We must revive this ancient tradition, for a people's democracy can only be built on mutual trust and co-operation.

This is the kind of structure we have to build – every village a state in essence, then larger states brought into being by a union of village states, and a world state brought into being by a union of regional states. In such a structure the village unit would have full autonomy. Only then can we establish the real and qualitative democracy, instead of present-day formal authoritative democracy.

The Indian government is very much under the influence of capitalism. They think there is no alternative to centralised production and distribution. This is true not only of the present government, but also of the communists. We plan to decentralise both production and distribution. But the communists do not countenance decentralisation. There is hardly any difference on this point between the capitalists and those who call themselves leftists, for they both accept centralised production by means of big machines. And because this is a central feature of capitalism, communists themselves might be called capitalists, at least in this regard.

Capitalism cannot be ended either by love or by conflict, but only by right thought. Conflict leads to ever more conflict. Love creates enthusiasm, but only right thought can initiate and effect a revolution. That is why we do not beg for gifts, but demand a share to which the poor are rightfully entitled. We want the people to understand and accept the idea that in a just and equitable order of society land must belong to all. We rely more than anything else on the force of this thought for furthering our cause. And yet if conflict becomes necessary we will deal with it nonviolently. Conflict is one of the factors of progress, but essentially it is the propagation of right thought which brings about revolution.

3
Social Justice

Persuading the rich to give

The task of redistributing the land by obtaining gifts is an act
of devotion and service, not only to the poor but also to the
rich – to all people. I have a strong conviction that this work is
going to have a general appeal. In the course of my begging, if
I happen to get less land at the place, I do not feel as if I have
received only a little. On the contrary, my feeling is that whatever I get is only a token of grace, and that ultimately God will
give with thousands of His hands, and my hands will prove
quite inadequate to receive. My present work is the preparation of a psychological climate.

People ask me when I shall complete my work. I do not
know. I am advanced in age and my body has been showing
signs of fatigue and exhaustion. By nature I have been a man
of the forest and a stranger to the ways of civilisation. I even
dreaded meeting great people. But nowadays I enter everybody's house unhesitatingly. This is all a miracle. In one place
in which I spent the whole day and delivered a speech before
the prayer audience I received only four acres. I returned to
my place and began my study of the *Upanishads*.Hardly ten
minutes passed before a villager came to me. He had neither
participated in the prayer nor heard my speech. "I have come
to donate land," he said. He had come six miles. He gave me
one acre out of his six. Scarcely had he turned his back when
another villager from a greater distance came and donated
fifty-two acres. In response to a day's work and a speech I got
only four acres. And here were donations without that effort.
What is it that influences the minds of people? Why should

man need the help of speech? A thought in the heart con-
ceived at home would do the work. But it is a stage which is yet
to come. For the present I speak and beg alms of land for the
poor.

Though my own stomach is very small, that of the poor is
very big. So if anyone asks me what my target is I say, "Fifty
million acres of land". If there are five sons in the family, I
want to be considered the sixth; if four, the fifth. Thus I claim
one-fifth or one-sixth of the total cultivable land in the country.

This will usher in an unprecedented and mighty revolution.
I can perceive it taking place before my eyes. People talk of the
Russian Revolution. That of the United States is an example of
another type. But looking at both these countries I find that
neither type of revolution is in accordance with the genius of
India, with our traditions and culture. I firmly believe that
India should be able to evolve, consistent with her ideals, a
new type of revolution based purely on love. If people begin to
donate lands of their own free will, readily and generously,
the whole atmosphere will undergo a sudden change and
India might well show the way to a new era of freedom, love
and happiness for the whole world. I therefore urge all of you,
whether you are a communist, a socialist, a conservative, or an
independent, to ponder this problem, and realise the value of
the Land Gift.

The corruption which we see around us is due to evils in the
present-day economy. People are swept away by the tide of
these outer evils and led to corruption. If we can change the
structure of economic life, Indian people will set a unique
example in the world. I hold to the belief that the moment we
succeed in creating a society free from exploitation, the intellectual and spiritual talent of the people of India, which lies
obscured at present, will shine. As a friend and well-wisher of
both the rich and the poor, I should feel happy only if I could
make the rich look upon the poor as members of their own
family. Unless the existing social order, which is based upon
inequality, strife and conflict, is replaced by equality and

mutual co-operation, there can be no salvation for mankind. In a society where some own land and others are landless there can be no peace. People wave legal documents to substantiate their claim to proprietorship. These serve no useful purpose. They tear our hearts and keep us divided. Let us burn them on the bonfire. People should accept the principle that all land belongs to God. If all land is socially owned, the present-day discontent will disappear and an era of love and co-operation take its place. My mission is not to stave off a revolution. I want to prevent a violent revolution and create a nonviolent revolution. The future peace and prosperity of the country depend upon the peaceful solution of the land problem. If land-owning people do not part with land, and a proper atmosphere for land reform is not created, the alternative is bloody revolution. I wish to prevent such a violent development, and I am convinced that peaceful methods can succeed. Land, like air, sun or water, is a free gift of God, and what I am asking for, on behalf of the landless, is no more than justice.

My aim is to bring about a threefold revolution. First, I want a change in people's hearts; secondly, I want to create a change in their lives; and thirdly, I want to change the social structure. Nothing can be achieved through pressure or force. If force is to be used, I am not required. My feeble hands are of little use. I am a humble servant with goodwill towards all. I have faith in the people. Everyone says that people do not want to part with land. Still, I have the courage to go about asking people to give it away. I go everywhere. I can go to a rich man's palace as well as to a poor man's hut.

I am an agent of the poor. I present their case. I have lived among them and have tried to make my life like theirs. But I want to be the big landlords' agent too, if they give generously to me. If they are liberal in giving away their land, I shall not have any hesitation in becoming their agent as well. It is highly inconsistent that those who possess land should not till it themselves, and those who cultivate it should not possess any. Those who cannot plough get it ploughed by others, while those who can have to do so as labourers. Since they have no right to the harvest they produce they work half-heartedly. Moreover, they do not even get sufficient food. Why should this be tolerated? Is it unjust to stop this false system? And am I doing a disservice to the landholder if, as a friend with full love for him, I ask him to donate fifty acres of his hundred? Is this not an indication of my genuine love for him? And if he insists on his old way of living, I reason with him saying that it is goodwill and friendliness towards a too-fat friend to advise him to reduce his weight, just as it is one's duty to persuade one who is too lean and emaciated to put on weight. A corpulent person has to make changes in his mode of living in order to slim.

I ask you to consider what could be God's plan. Can His plan permit some to possess land and others nothing? The land that you have acquired from others should be returned to them, even though today you are its owner. I do not want arithmetical equality, but I do want equity, or such equality as, for instance, the five fingers of the hand have. These five fingers are not equal in size, but they all work in full co-operation and together perform innumerable tasks. Again, their inequality is not disproportionate as it would be if, say, the smallest finger were an inch in length, while the largest one was a foot. The moral is that even if there cannot be absolute equality, there should also not be disproportionate inequality. There should be equity. The five fingers possess different powers. Similarly each man possesses a different capacity. All inherent capacities should be developed.

My argument that every son of the soil has a right to Mother Earth is not my own. The *Vedas* proclaim it. No brother can prevent another brother from serving his mother. And I even say that whoever demands land must have it and it is the duty of the landlords to give it to him. Is drinking water denied when asked for? And if someone denies it, how ashamed he looks! Similarly one should feel ashamed to refuse to give land to one who asks for it. I can understand that one should not give food to another without asking him to labour for it. But if one demands the means to do that labour, it is our duty to provide him with them. It is also the duty of the government to allot land to the needy at the rate of five acres per family.

I desire to humiliate neither the poor nor the rich. So if a great landlord donates a few acres, I decline to accept his gift for that would be to humiliate the poor. But my experience has been that if people are properly persuaded they give a sufficient donation. To cite one incident: a landlord owning three hundred acres came and offered me one acre. I declined to accept his gift. On explaining to him my point of view, he unreservedly raised his donation to thirty acres. It took hardly two minutes to persuade him. If I had been asking for donations for the erection of a temple I would have been satisfied with an acre. But I ask for land as a right of the poor. I do not beg alms. If I gave the poor cooked food instead of land it would certainly be humiliating to them. As a thirsty man is not humiliated if he asks for and accepts water, so the landless is not humiliated by accepting land. Rather, he must be thanked for accepting the donation. For a mere acceptance of land will not give him crops. It is only when he puts in hard labour that he reaps the harvest. So the recipient has no reason to harbour any inferiority complex.

I am generating a spirit of nonviolent revolt in the people by making them land-hungry. At present property and possession are the order of the day, the ruling principle the world over. What is more, an imposing legal framework has been raised around it, giving it the appearance of respectability, and therefore it does not strike one as wrong. We consider stealing to be a crime, but connive at those who encourage this anti-social activity by amassing heaps of money themselves. As we know, it is the miser who gives rise to the thief. We condemn thieves to rot in prison, but let their creators roam about in complete freedom. They even occupy seats of honour and respectability in society.

4
Peace

Freedom from arms

What country in the world is free today? Is America a free country, or England, India or Pakistan, China or Japan? The mark of a free country is that it can plan its life independently, but what country now makes independent plans? It is obvious that although America is far from weak in military matters, she nevertheless feels weak. She feels that her armed forces are not strong enough by comparison with Russia's, and so a bill is introduced in Congress to increase the military budget. Does America then make independent plans? It is Russia who is making plans for America. What kind of freedom is this? Nor is Russia independent. She says she has been surrounded by American bases and will have to make more and more new weapons. The Soviet expenditure on arms is determined by America.

Russia says America has dangerous ideas and so she has to increase her armaments. America says exactly the same thing about Russia. The government of China says that it must spend money on increasing its army and armaments because of its fear of India, Russia or America. The government of India says that it must pay attention to the army because of the undesirable tendencies in Pakistan or China.

This will continue as long as the peoples of the world are burdened by governments. Government means that a handful of men feel that they are responsible for the safety of millions of people, and those people also feel that these men are their protectors. The result is that their minds are never free from fear, and where fear rules, men rely on force, on the army.

And the more they put their faith in the army, the greater becomes their fear.

If India today is bold enough to reduce its armies, its real strength will be greatly increased. Pakistan and China will no longer waste resources on maintaining their armies. This step demands courage, it is not for cowards. We are cowards, and cowards have no imagination. Do we really think anyone is going to attack us? Other nations are making atom and hydrogen bombs. We possess no bombs, so we think we should at least have a penknife! I believe that if India would reduce her army, she could become the strongest nation in the world, and her moral authority would be greatly increased. Such a step would win the hearts of the people.

India is a large country, with a big population. But size does not necessarily make us strong. Neither does the possession of a strong army make a country strong. True strength resides in the character of the people, and progress depends upon the improvement in the quality of life of the people.

The people are dependent upon the government. They pay taxes for the upkeep of an army and imagine that they are safe. But they are not safe, so long as they are not fearless – so long as they rely upon the army and feel unable to defend themselves. The people have become soft – they sleep long hours, they are afraid to get wet in the rain or to work in the sun. Suppose we were at war, and news were to be received that our army had had a set-back, they would lose heart at once and panic. A nation of cowards cannot be saved by its army. Every man, woman and child must have fearlessness, and life must become less soft and more rigorous. An army is no substitute for fearlessness, a hospital is no substitute for compassion, and a college is no substitute for a love of knowledge. National security does not depend upon the army, it depends upon the fearlessness of the people.

Violence has grown to such huge proportions nowadays that it no longer has the power to solve the world's problems. The most prosperous and advanced countries, those that lack for nothing, tremble with fear at one another. They sit down to talk things over amicably round a table, but all the time they are getting ready the strongest possible armies and armaments. As a consequence no progress is made. The whole world is darkened by fear, and not a single problem gets any nearer to a solution. Men will be compelled in the end to take refuge in nonviolence. Violence seems to be all-powerful at present, but in fact it is at the point of death. Just before a lamp goes out its flame flares up, and that is what is happening to violence, its fires are about to go out. Mankind is hungering and thirsting for peace, and feels a great longing that the problems of society should be solved by methods of peace, compassion and friendliness.

All these big bombs, these armaments, are going to come to an end. And how? The very hands that made them will destroy them. All these swords and guns are going to go back to the factories where they were made to be melted down and turned into ploughshares. All these steel weapons will be thrown into the melting pot, and be transformed into useful tools – sickles and ploughs and spades – by the very workers who once made armaments. And when? When our ways of thought are changed. When a revolution in thought takes place, a new world arises on the ruins of the old. When the sun rises, the same people who a few hours previously have spread out their sleeping mats, get up and roll them up. In the same way, as soon as those who are manufacturing armaments realise that these things cannot solve any of our problems, they will themselves destroy them. What happens in an earthquake? The bigger the house the sooner it falls.

Nowadays nonviolence has come to mean that society should be disturbed as little as possible. Social life should not be upset, our present set-up should continue to function without hindrance – that is all that we mean by nonviolence. It is said that a 'socialistic pattern' should be worked out; at the same time it is said that the methods adopted should be 'nonviolent'. A number of people understand them to mean merely that the changes necessary to the 'socialistic pattern' will be carried out with extreme gradualness. People imagine that nonviolence means that we should go to work as cautiously as a man who has a boil or some other injury on his hand, and wants to avoid making it ache by any sudden exertion. Let there be no painful, sudden changes. So nonviolence is rendered innocuous.

We cannot go far ahead, things remain pretty much as they are. At the same time we have the satisfaction of adopting an ideal, paying it lip service, and talking about it. This conception appears to me to be very dangerous to the cause of nonviolence, and very convenient to the cause of violence. The lord Buddha put the thing very clearly: "If we are lethargic in doing good, evil grows with the greater speed."

Therefore it is not in the interests of nonviolence to equate it with an avoidance of trouble by reducing to the minimum the rate of social change. If you 'go-slow', evil propensities have great strength. So I beg of you not to adopt any 'go-slow' methods in nonviolence. Apply them to violence by all means – that is all to the good – but in nonviolence you must go full steam ahead. If you want the good to come speedily, you must go about it with vigour. A merely soft, spineless, ineffective kind of 'nonviolence' will actually encourage the growth of those forces of violence which we deplore.

It is very dangerous that nonviolence should move slowly. Then it turns into a conservative force, a preserver of the status quo, and this is a matter to which we should give serious thought. We must understand that nonviolence is a direct way to revolution in the mind of man and in society. If nonviolence does not bring revolution, consider, it is not nonviolence, it may be lack of violence, or it may be violence in hiding. Nonviolence is a forceful way to eliminate exploitation and bring justice.

Peace soldiers

The fundamental problem of the whole world today is the

establishment of peace. Perhaps in no other age has there been such hunger for peace. Even the countries whose whole way of thought was deeply dyed with violence, today long to find release from it. It is true that they go on increasing their armaments, but nevertheless they are wondering how to get rid of them. People have come to understand that arms achieve nothing. All progress in real welfare is blocked by the immense expenditure of resources on the army. In former days the weapons were in the hands of men; this is no longer so, men are now in the hands of their weapons. Should the spark of war now set the world on fire, no man could control it. Mankind has, therefore, lost faith in the possibility of solving its problems through war or violence. If arms can no longer settle our disputes, then some other way of settling them must be found. I am therefore proposing the formation of Shanti Sena - a Peace Army.

We will not be able to bring about a revolution by peaceful methods unless the people feel at the same time that our ideas offer them a powerful means of self-defence even in our present state of affairs. These distinctions between high and low, rich and poor, are a cause of unrest and violence. If they are got rid of, there is no doubt that unrest will also disappear. We have blazed a trail, and pointed it out to the people – the replacement of individual ownership by community ownership and by co-operative, constructive work. It is, therefore, necessary for the healthy growth of the process of peaceful revolution in which we are already engaged that we should make ourselves responsible for peace.

At the time of war there will be some who will undertake to nurse the wounded soldiers. These men are full of love and sympathy and compassion for living beings. They do not make any distinction between friend and foe and volunteer to go to the front at risk to their lives. They serve the sick and the wounded. There is no doubt that they are kind and their services are valuable. Nevertheless, it should be clearly recognised that their service cannot contribute to the abolition of evil war. Their kindness is only an aspect of a society which believes in war. Just as wheels in a machine, working apparently in different and even contrary directions, are nonetheless parts of that machine contributing to the total operation, so the killing of living soldiers and the nursing of the wounded are both parts of the war-machine. Only appearances are different. Evidently one is a cruel job and the other is kind. However, both the cruelty of the cruel and the kindness of the kind go to make up the war-machine. To be scientifically true and frank, so long as we recognise war as legitimate, both the doctor who undertakes to treat the wounded and the soldier who kills are on the same footing. Both are guilty of war. This means that by mere acts of kindness we cannot hope to create the kingdom of kindness; that is, the kingdom where kindness will rule. We do not aim at doing acts of kindness but at creating a kingdom of kindness. Kindness can and does exist even in the kingdom of wickedness, but only as a pinch of salt does in food – kind acts only add to the taste of that with which they are mixed. Such kindness brings a sort of flavour to the violence of war, it cannot end war. So if we merely indulge in such acts of kindness, as will make of it a handmaid to wickedness, acting in obedience to the latter, we will not have done our real work. We must therefore develop a longer view and desist from undertaking any activity merely because it appears to be a constructive act of service.

Nonviolence is not going to succeed until it shows itself able to bring together the strength of many minds to bear on one point with one united purpose. Let there be many kinds of mind, and let there be a pooling of minds. At present nonviolence does not display this power, and violence does. The result is that although there are very few people today who have any fundamental faith in violence, they do respect it to a certain extent because it proves effective in getting things done. Violence retains this respect, even though people have already lost faith in it. If nonviolence cannot show the same power of organisation which violence possesses, it is not going to succeed, except in the individual field. Those individuals who have developed nonviolent strength have been effective in the past and will be so in the future. But in society at large nonviolence can only succeed if it can show the power to unite, to organise and to plan.

Nonviolence is unable to display this power because it has certain limitations, and these very limitations derive from its characteristic qualities. One of these characteristics is that nonviolence cannot *impose* its demands. It can only explain its ideas and must leave men free to accept them or not. Let us suppose that tomorrow a nonviolent government were to come into power. It might put forward a proposition: "This year we shall need to spend such an amount." It would then go on to suggest a scale of giving, so that no one need find it a burden: "Let a man with an income of a thousand pounds give so much, with ten thousand so much." They would explain: "People may give more if they wish, but if they give on this scale the budget will be met, and we shall be able to provide the nation with the services we desire." If they were to explain why a budget of this size is necessary, and then ask for gifts, what would you expect to happen? Would they get more than by taxation? If the government has been genuinely chosen by the people, if it listens to their grievances and sets them right, and then puts the budget before the people and asks for gifts, why should it not get what it needs? We shall only get a nonviolent State when the government is able to ask for gifts and get more than it could by taxation. Until then, nonviolence will not succeed.

Nonviolence cannot compel anyone. It gives complete freedom. Nonviolence means that every individual is free to obey orders, or to disregard them, and that he obeys of his own free will. When that happens a nonviolent state can be established. The testing-point of nonviolence is this – that the people so trust the word of the leaders of the nonviolent society that they accept it as completely binding upon them. Nonviolence will come when orders are carried out without 'orders', when an influence spreads without 'influence'.

Nonviolence suggests, it does not command, but its suggestions are more powerful than any commands. It is not going to grow beyond its infancy until the Peace Soldiers report for duty at any given point as soon as the need is proclaimed.

We have still to understand the idea of 'disciplined obedience'. There is a reason for our slowness in doing so, and that is the egoism in men of 'good nature'. In the nonviolent movement, the proportion of 'good' individuals is comparatively large. These 'good' people hold very firmly to their various opinions. This strength of conviction, however, carries with it its corresponding defect. Men of strong principles are prone to a certain amount of pride, a defect which is the accompanying 'shadow' of their good qualities. When a 'good' man possesses humility, this may be accompanied by the fault of vacillation, the shadow of that virtue. In the world as we know it there is no such thing as a virtue without its shadow. We cannot have light without darkness, sun without shade. Just as we cannot have a picture without the marks of the drawing, so we cannot have any quality without its defect – the quality inevitably carries its shadow with it, and as the shadow reveals the form of the quality, I do not think of the shadow as a defect. Take my own case. People do not know how lazy I really am because I keep on travelling. But my aspirations to non-attachment in the spiritual life are all mixed up with laziness. If someone asks me the wrong sort of question I am naturally inclined to return a sharp answer, but thanks to my laziness I do not answer at all. Thanks to this laziness, nonviolence and non-attachment have a natural attraction for me. It seems to me that if I were to tell a lie I should have to get involved in a great many pretences and a great many machinations in order to support the lie. But if I tell the plain and simple truth everything is easy – I need do nothing. If I get angry, I must roll my eyes, shake my fist and say something or other; if I don't get angry, I need do nothing at all. Labour is reduced to a minimum.

People sometimes ask why these 'good' people cannot agree among themselves. Those 'bad' ones do unite, their associations flourish; why not the associations of 'good' folk also? The reason is that it is so difficult for 'good' people to get rid of this pride. In order to achieve the qualities of 'good' without pride, knowledge of the Self is essential, nothing else can overcome pride.

A Peace Soldier must be prepared to accept and fulfil the following:

That he believes in the principles of truth, nonviolence, non-possessiveness, manual labour, and self-control.

That he believes that the world can only know true peace when the common people are in direct control of their own affairs. He will, therefore, not take any part in party politics or power-politics.

That he will devote his whole mind to disinterested service of the people. That he will give no place in his life to any spirit of exclusiveness in matters of caste, class or religion.

That he will give his whole time and his best thought to the work of the nonviolent revolution.

That whenever and wherever he may be ordered to go for the work of the Peace Army, he shall be prepared to go and also, should need arise, to give his life in this service.

What is the importance of the requirement that a Peace Soldier may not be a member of any political party? Why should he be non-partisan and stay away from the burden of politics?

I desire only to point out that even the soldiers of the armed forces are expected to keep aloof from party politics. It is recognised even in military circles that the soldier must be the servant of *all*. When such is the case, it is surely absolutely essential for the Peace Soldier to keep the pledge about remaining free from all party entanglements.

Consider the outbreaks of violence which often take place. A caste quarrel between 'untouchables' and 'higher' castes took place in south India. In addition, the untouchables were mainly Christian, and the higher castes Hindu, so that Hindu-Christian rivalry came into it. One political party espoused the cause of one side, and another political party took up the other side, consequently the division became political. So in this cord of strife three strands were twisted together – religion, caste and politics. If the Peace Soldiers who go there belong to a political party they can do no work at all as political differences are one of the causes of strife. Just as the Peace Soldier observes no caste distinctions and regards all religions with the same respect, so he must take care to keep out of party politics.

The man who is to stand up for the service of the whole community must have no favourites and must be devoted to truth. He must have the courage to speak out, no matter who is at fault. No party member can do that because he is bound by party discipline. We must not only be free of party ties, we must be committed to destroying the party system, and to do this we must set an example ourselves of non-party organisation.

The pledge that the Peace Soldier must submit to a commander is not really inconsistent with what I have been saying about an 'anarchist' society and about freedom of thought, although it may appear to be contradictory. In its other aspects, the Peace Army is quite the opposite of all other armies; but as regards discipline its standards cannot be less strict than theirs, in fact they have to be more strict. For in this army there is no question of taking life. The armed soldier also may lose his own life, and he takes that risk; because of that, an aura of heroism surrounds his calling. The work of the Peace Army, however, is entirely one-sided; it is a matter of losing one's own life, but of saving the lives of others. If a man comes at me with a sword, I must not be thinking at all of protecting my own throat against the attack, but only of how to protect him against any possible injury. The standard that I look for cannot possibly be reached without discipline.

No one should judge anyone else, or order him to become a

Peace Soldier. This is a matter to be decided in the man's own heart. It is a step that must be taken with care. For it involves much greater strength and fearlessness. Suppose that some dreadful incident were to take place somewhere and that fasting is the only way to solve the problem. A Peace Soldier feels that he must perform an act of purification. On such occasions, if you ask me what is involved in taking up the Command, I would say that it means accepting the responsibility, should the need arise, of a fast unto death.

A nonviolent command is nothing but a command to self-sacrifice. All the rest is very trivial by comparison. The word command is appropriate, but the first act of the commander, whether great or small, is the offering of himself.

A fear can be expressed that this is a regimentation of thought which will constitute a threat to freedom, and that even though at first it is confined to the Peace Army, it may spread later to other fields. We should do the work which naturally comes to us, even though there may be faults in it. There is some risk in every new beginning. But we must be clear in our minds about the field within which orders can be given and obeyed. With regard to knowledge, orders are impossible. In the field of thought there must indeed be complete freedom.

Nonviolence, if it is to be effective, must have the same ability as violence now possesses, to bring pressure to bear at a particular point. In the end, when the mental, material and social revolution has been completed, this question will not arise; there will be no problem at all. But today, while the problems exist, the advocates of violence can get together thousands and thousands of men at a moment's notice.

Nonviolence is based on voluntary obedience which is not an easy thing. But we may hope that some day nonviolence will take the place of violence if only, somehow, we succeed in the difficult task of combining free will with obedience. Otherwise the armed forces will continue to carry the responsibility for public defence, and all that nonviolence will be able to do will be alleviate the harshness of life in various ways. Even a violent society recognises that life ought to have a pleasant flavour, and nonviolence has the power to introduce this sweet savour. Even a society whose tutelary deity is violence recognises that to nurse the wounded is a work of mercy. That much of love, nonviolence and compassion is respected even in a violent community. But as we have seen, we expect much more of nonviolence than this; our task demands that we should be able to bring hundreds of people together, to one place and for one purpose, in an orderly way.

The organisation of the armed forces is entirely different. They are kept together in one place, they are given special training, they become machines. Care is taken that no ideas from outside shall touch them, so that no differences of opinion may arise. But in our plan, it is the duty of the Peace Soldiers to make themselves familiar with whatever ideas are current in the world, they are expected to bring an alert mind and a free and independent judgement to the study and analysis of such ideas, and they are free to accept or reject any of them. They are not to keep aloof from knowledge of any sort.

Our organisation will be quite different from that of the armed forces. Suppose we were to be asked to make a plan for the whole of India, we would choose an all-India group of fifteen to twenty persons who have complete faith in the power of peace, who apply this faith in their lives, who practise daily self-examination and constant self-correction, and who have a measure of purity of mind. If such an all-India 'Peace Command' could be established, it would have a big influence.

Our imagined all-India 'Peace Command' would not issue any orders, but it would give advice to those who sought it. It would also occasionally give advice without being asked. Its second task would be to send Peace Soldiers to any part of the country where violence takes place, or any disturbance of the peace. It would make inquiries into the truth of the situation and collect the facts at once.

Let us suppose that a soldier needs some outside help for the work that he is doing in his particular field. If he does not want help there is no problem – in that case he is his own master, he does his own work, he is self-sufficient. But there may be occasions when someone needs outside help, and in that case help must be sent at once. There must be no delay, and those who are sent must be humble-minded people. When we go into someone else's area of work, we cannot go there in the spirit of a doctor who has come to set things right. Those who go must be ready to obey the orders of the man who works there, to work in harmony with him. There must be some agency to give him orders and send him to the spot.

This command of the Peace Army is like the command of the guru. If there were no guru, the word of command would be like a widow. It is not any other man's word of command that is effective but only that of the guru. For in the guru is wisdom, love and truth, and no shadow of violence. Where all these qualities are found, the word of command is never slighted. In this kind of surrender of self-will there is no compulsion; a man is not compelled to it from without, he is impelled to it from within. It is thus a spontaneous impulse to desire that the guru's word be law.

If you are told that the way to swim is not to stand up in the river but to lie flat, would you get so much into the habit of lying flat that you would continue to lie flat when you came out on to the bank? The rule about lying flat is limited to the river. When you get to the bank you must stand up. It is only a man who is free in every department of life who will be able to obey orders in the Peace Army. If someone is so stupid and slavish that on every occasion he hangs his head and never thinks for himself, he will never be able to obey a command of this sort. The man who has fallen into the habit of slavery will prove incapable of obedience when the right time comes.

Jesus Christ made use of this word 'command'. At the end of his life he said to his disciples: "Love one another – a new commandment I have given to you" – that is his language.

Now just see what this means. When such a faith is born, man needs no external spur – he spurs himself. So there is nothing in the Peace Army to hinder independence of thought.

It is not necessary to appoint leaders in different places, but if one is available, this is a matter for rejoicing. Such a guide may not always be available, and there may not always be a need for him. You keep a dictionary by you for reference, and you do not find it a nuisance. The dictionary will not tell you of itself what word to use. You will have to do your own thinking. But whenever you need it, you can refer to it. In the same way, when you have a guide available, it only means that you have someone to turn to.

It is better for a Peace Soldier to wear ordinary clothes. If he were to put on a special uniform it would have an adverse effect on those he desires to serve. People would regard him as someone set apart, and Soldiers must *not* be in any way separated from society. He must be a man whom people will not hesitate to ask for help whenever they need it; and there is a risk that a special uniform would be a hindrance to this intimacy. It is most important that he should not be cut off from the community.

Only he who serves all men with the spirit of a mother can become a Peace Soldier. There are many instances of brother saving brother, friend saving friend, a servant saving his master. But the most wonderful of all is the mother who saves her children in danger, and this happens not only among human beings but also among animals. If a tigress's cubs are captured, how she springs to their rescue, even though she knows that she will be killed by the rifle of the hunter. Her struggle to save her cubs ends only with her death and she has no fear of her opponents.

Our government builds up an army. What is the moral basis of that army? It is the sanction of the nation's vote. Without that the army would be nothing but a gang of armed robbers. But the sanction of the vote is a very weak one, for it is a majority vote only in name. Sixty per cent of the population have voted, and thirty per cent of them have voted for the government party. The remaining thirty per cent have divided their votes between various other parties, and the government is run by the party with the thirty per cent backing. In countries where this 'democratic' system is in operation, governments elected by thirty per cent exercise power over a hundred per cent of the people. But they are supposed to hold the people's mandate, and so the army is accepted as a national army.

Our Peace Army needs to have a spiritual authority behind it. If we were to enter on this path without people's consent, our steps would have no strength. We need the general consent of the community which we propose to serve. For after all our aim is not merely to sacrifice our own lives, our aim is the establishment of a just order among the people. We therefore need the consent of the people because we need the authority not merely to serve, but to bring a moral influence to bear upon them. The votes which are given nowadays to political parties do not imply any action. The Peace Army does not want that kind of consent. It does not want you to hand over to us the responsibility for your protection. If you did that, we should be the protectors, and the rest of the population protected. If we were to work on that basis, we should be creating a new caste.

We therefore do not ask for a vote to give us the right to protect you; we ask a pledge that you approve of our programme and will join us in carrying it out. As a symbol of this every family of five persons should give every year one hank of yarn, or something corresponding, something produced by the giver's own labour. In the *Sarvodaya Patra* (keeping a gift vessel for the Peace Army and putting a handful of grain in every day) we shall understand that the spiritual strength and moral consent of the giver is behind us in our work.

The government is backed by the power of taxation. People recognise its right, as their own elected government, to impose and collect taxes. We also need a voluntary tax; the *Sarvodaya Patra* represents a voluntary tax for the support of our work. There are seventy million families in India; if we can get this kind of voluntary support even from ten million of them, it will be a very big thing. We will then have created in India a kind of strength that has never been seen before, anywhere in the world. If ten million people freely give a handful of grain before every meal, our work will receive an access of power such as has never and nowhere been known before. Once we can achieve this broad basis of support, we will have the deciding voice in the national councils, no matter what party is in power and whether we have any share in the government or not. No party will ever be able to lay claim to such solid support as the Peace Army will have received. Party politicians ask for the votes only once in five years, but the people will be giving us their vote daily with their handful of grain. If we can implant this idea of a daily gift of grain, we need not trouble to get political power; the reality of power will be ours.

The special feature of the *Sarvodaya Patra* is that it gives us not only material support, but a spiritual fellowship of friends.

Suppose two violent men, who believe in violent methods, are fighting each other, is it our duty to intervene between them? Nonviolence has certain limits within which it can be effective. It is probable that we could do nothing by interfering in a fight between men of violent principles. All the same, when a nonviolent man is in touch with them, or sees a murderous conflict going on before his eyes, it is his duty to intervene. When a fire has broken out, the water does not ask whether it lies within its power to quench it. It sets to work. If the water is effective the fire will go out; if not, the water will evaporate and the fire go on burning.

Those who enlist in the Peace Army will consider it their duty to serve the whole human community, without regard for caste, religion, sect, party or any other distinctions. The Peace Soldier must treat everyone, high or low, in the same way; like water he must be humble, gentle, clean, pure and cool. So gentle is water that it can touch even the eye and cause no pain, yet so strong that it can crack open the very rocks. Its special virtue is that it does not attack the obstacle in its path; if it cracks the rock, the rock is responsible. The water is broken up by the rock and scattered into drops, but that does not harm the water; it may appear to be shattered, but it does not die, it lives in every drop. Water is humble, yet in the end it is the rock that breaks. Like water, the Peace Soldier must be very humble.

There is no place in the Peace Army for the faint-hearted and the fearful. Its work is for the fearless and stout-hearted. Only the brave can join it. The Peace Army has no use for those who think too much of their bodies, who cannot discipline their minds or control their anger. It is the glory of the brave to endure, to be patient, to forgive. Forgiveness, endurance and patience are not commonplace matters, they demand courage. There is no courage in the lust to kill, to shed blood in anger. And as for the coward who turns his back and runs away, and longs for someone to save him, he is not nonviolent. Inwardly, if not outwardly, he is a shedder of blood. A truly nonviolent man is fearless. A cat behaves like a tiger towards a mouse, but it behaves like a mouse towards a dog. A tiger confronted by a deer is bold enough but it is scared when confronted by a gun. This sort of behaviour is the mark of a coward, and cowards have no place in the Peace Army.

It must not be thought that the Peace Soldier has work to do only when fighting actually breaks out. He must give himself day in and day out to work for the service of the people. The work of peace-making can only be done by those who have already found their way into people's hearts and captured their affections by the services they have performed. Those who have not laboured as servants of the people and won their love cannot be effective. As a servant of the people he will be busy even when there is no prospect of violence. He will not sit idle in times of peace; there should be no need for him to resort to 'physical jerks' in order to digest his food. He will be busy all day long helping the children, the aged, the sick of the community. He will always be ready to listen to the people's troubles. Naturally, he will not be able to solve all their problems, but he will comfort them by his sympathy, and he will bring the difficulties of particular individuals to the notice of the community and try to find a remedy with the help of all. He will do his utmost to prevent disputes within the community from being taken to court. He will find this work to be a full-time job.

Man experiences love from birth to death, everywhere and at every moment. It may be said that man is born in love, dies in love, and is absorbed into love. So wide is his experience of love, and yet the power of love has not been developed. Why is this? Why does this power not grow? It is because our love is merely 'reciprocal', that is, we only love those who love us. This is a thing which even animals do. If you offer a cow some fresh green grass, she will come to you affectionately; she sees your love for her and reciprocates it. But there is no strength in this love; strength only comes when 'aggressive' love is shown. If a man hates us, and we love him all the same, that is a source of power. A child loves his mother. The mother suckles him, and the child responds to the mother's loving service by giving her his love in return. In this way love is born of love, but there is no power in it. Hate breeds hate, love breeds love, fear breeds fear, just as goats breed goats and sheep breed sheep. Love of one's own kind is reciprocated but it is merely a case of like breeding like. It is the ordinary nature of love that love should call forth love in response. If an object is placed before a mirror, the reflection of that object appears in the mirror. The mirror does not create a picture, it merely shows a reflection. So, when someone loves us and we return his love, our love is merely a reflection of his. The power of love is revealed when we are confronted by hatred and still show love. The strength of love is shown when we love our enemies.

The great nations fear one another and think one another to be in the wrong. Instead of experimenting with love in the face of hatred, they consider that such a thing is impractical. But if we want to build up the power of love, we have to learn the art of meeting hatred with love, and demonstrate it convincingly.

We are now living in the scientific age, and this age demands a subtle and far-reaching revolution in the heart of man. For it is possible now for a man to sit in his house and set the whole world on fire; and it must also be possible to discover the nonviolent power which will enable a man to sit in his house and give the whole world peace. We must now see what form this search should take.

Imagine that on this side there are a hundred angry men, and on that side there are fifty men who are also feeling angry, but who believe in nonviolence and so are keeping their anger under control. Which group do you suppose has the greater moral power? Imagine further that there are five men who feel no anger at all, but whose hearts are filled with universal love and compassion. Tell me, which of these three groups has the greatest strength? It is clear that though the five men are few in number, the change in their moral outlook gives them superior strength. Now if there should be a single man who feels his identity with all, and looks upon everyone as his friend, he will have greater strength even than these five. The more a homoeopathic medicine is concentrated, and the smaller its size, the more powerful it becomes. Nonviolence works in the same way. In this age of science, sharp weapons cannot help us. Only the gentlest possible *Satyagraha* (force of truth) will yield results. This means that the purer are our motives and attitudes, the stronger our Peace Army will be. We certainly need numbers but the most important thing is this purity of attitude. It is that which will make the Peace Army strong.

We are challenged by the fact that the government has to keep an army at all. The first and greatest challenge to workers for nonviolence is the army itself; all the rest is secondary. The way to answer this challenge which confronts us is to demonstrate that we have the power to keep the peace within our own borders. It will have its effect in the international field also. Successful work for peace at home will give us a clue to how the idea of peace can be worked out in the international field, and it will also bring us the opportunity for such work. But so long as we cannot keep the peace in our internal affairs, we shall get no chance to work out the idea in international relations, nor shall we have any clue as to how it may be done. This is the challenge and the opportunity which confront us.

In the age of science, when the task is to bring the whole world together into unity, the time for the nation states is over. In the past they have fulfilled a useful purpose by joining men together into nations and kingdoms and creating the spirit of national community. But the demand of our own time is to bring an end to the nation states. Nation states are out of date.

Science may be defined as knowledge of the natural universe. This knowledge is acquired by the study and contemplation of creation. This contemplation of creation leads to science, while the contemplation of the Creator leads to spiritual knowledge. We have to study both the creation and the Creator, but the study of creation has to be made under the guidance of spiritual knowledge. In a motor car there are two pieces of machinery which are necessary for driving, the steering-wheel and the accelerator. We may think of spiritual knowledge as the steering-wheel and of science as the accelerator. Science increases the speed of our lives, but spiritual knowledge ensures that they go in the right direction. Both are necessary for progress.

You must get rid of the divisive spirit of 'I' and 'mine'. If you do not rise above these distinctions, you can make no spiritual progress, achieve no personal happiness, attain no peace of mind. But in these days science, too, is saying exactly the same thing. If you cling to your petty egoisms, and your petty possessiveness, there is no hope for you, you will experience complete destruction. In the conflict between man and man, between one power and another, both will be destroyed. Thus, when science and spiritual wisdom are saying the same thing, it is essential that this wisdom should be made part of the common life of society.

That self-knowledge whose source was in the solitary place where the guru sat with his disciple must now enter every home. When these two are yoked together, they will bring a Heaven on earth; otherwise there will be universal destruction. In the past the call for the renunciation of egoism has come from the spiritual traditions, and has aimed at the salvation of the individual. But now, this renunciation of egoism has become necessary for the salvation of society. Science is warning the human race that unless we give up our egoism and unite, we cannot survive. The call to the individual to give up his egoism for the sake of his soul's welfare, and in order to attain heaven, was one that appealed to comparatively few. Today, the very survival of the race depends on our learning to base our lives on self-knowledge. It has become a 'historical necessity', it is essential for modern society, and the Peace Army must make it a reality.

The armed forces go on drilling even in normal times, in times of peace. In exactly the same way the Peace Army will in normal times be continuously engaged in spreading self-knowledge and the Peace Soldier will maintain his contacts with every home in the area, to bring spiritual understanding to the people. This kind of service has to be spread throughout the country, and the result ought to be that wherever there is a Peace Soldier a breach of the peace will be unknown. Not merely will there be an absence of violence, but the people will feel positive kindliness towards one another.

5
Spiritual Consciousness

To understand one's *'svadharma'*, one's natural state of being, one's true self, is the most important thing in life. Only in our natural and normal state of being can we find fulfilment. We do not adopt *svadharma* because it is noble or cast it off because it is base. It is neither great nor small. It is equal to our measure. Each individual has his own distinct *dharma*. In a community of two hundred there are two hundred different *dharma*. My *dharma* today is not what it was ten years ago; it will not be the same in ten years' time. Experience transforms one's *dharma*.

Another's *dharma* may appear *superior* but I cannot adopt it. The sun with its warmth and light may appear a more attractive place than this dull earth but as I am not built to withstand its heat I could never live there. If I say to a fish, "Milk is more luxurious than water. Come and swim in this milk", will it accept? In milk a fish will die.

Another's *dharma* may appear *easier* but I cannot adopt it. A family man who gives up the world to escape his children and avoid his *svadharma* gets caught in his hypocrisy. He runs from life's burdens to the forest. Since asceticism is not his *svadharma* the first thing he does is build a hut. Then he puts up a fence to protect it. It appears that he has escaped from his household but he has built new burdens.

For the man whose mind is truly detached renunciation is not difficult. It is a matter of vocation. High or low, easy or difficult, inner growth must be real and fulfilment genuine.

Svadharma is natural. One does not have to go out looking for it. I did not drop from the sky but was born into a stream of existence. Society, parents, neighbours, all existed before I was born. To serve the parents who gave me life, to serve the society that succoured me is my vocation from birth. *Svadharma*, like one's mother, is not chosen but pre-determined. No matter what sort of person she is, there is no denying her motherhood. To disown one's *svadharma* is to disown oneself, to commit suicide. Only in harmony with it can we move forward. That is why we should never lose sight of it.

Our *svadharma* should come easily and naturally but because of illusions this does not happen. The common factor in our illusions is a shallow identification of oneself with one's body. I, and those related to me through the body, set the limits of my expansion. Those outside the circle are strangers or enemies. Identifying ourselves with the body we start putting up all sorts of little walls. Almost everyone does this. One man's enclosure may be larger than another's but all surround themselves with a wall. It is no thicker than their skin. One man's enclosure is the family, another's the nation. One wall divides the middle from the working classes, another divides Christians from Hindus. In this way many walls have been erected. Wherever you turn you see nothing but walls.

Determination to realise one's *svadharma* is not enough. There are two other principles: "I am not this mortal body; the body is only the outer covering" and "I am the spirit that never dies, that cannot be reduced, that pervades everything". Aware of the transience of the body and the indestructibility of the spirit, *svadharma* will not seem hard, in fact, anything not *svadharma* will be difficult.

Look! This body is for ever changing, caught in the cycle of childhood, youth and old age. Every seven years it is renewed. Not a drop of old blood remains. This body that changes every moment, dies every moment. Twenty-four hours a day its sewers operate, but despite indefatigable scavenging it remains unclean. Is this body you? It is dirty; it is you who wash it. It is sick; it is you who treat it with medicine. It fills three cubits of space; you live in three worlds (of body, mind and spirit). It changes endlessly; you observe these changes. It is open to death; you accept it. When the distinction between your body and yourself is so clear why do you say that only that which relates to the body belongs to you? And why grieve for the death of the body?

We hate the word 'death'. It seems bad luck to mention it. If someone dies, what tears! What mourning! Even when death is imminent we do not tell the patient. The doctor may tell us, but we say nothing. And he, unable to speak plainly, pours and pumps in drugs as long as there is breath in the body. If, instead, he were to tell the patient the truth he could give him courage and direct his thoughts towards God. What a help that would be! It is feared that this brittle pot might crack of shock before its time. Could it crack before the right moment? Besides, if it is due to crack in two hours and cracks now, what difference does it make? This does not mean one should become hard-hearted and loveless. But attachment to the body is not love. On the contrary, unless attachment to the body is overcome, true love does not emerge.

We have forgotten that life is to be lived for the realisation of *svadharma*, and to do this one has to foster and cherish the body. This does not just mean satisfying the palate. We do not eat to titillate the tongue but to feed the body. The body is an instrument which has its roots in the spirit. If we lose ourselves in it we stunt our spirit, and the body, which has little intrinsic value, is made of less worth. Attachment to the body and to those to whom we are related is wrong if it means we give nothing of ourselves to anyone other than a close relative or friend. Do we make any effort to let soul mingle with soul, self meet self? Do we let the bird of the spirit escape from this cage and breathe freedom? Does it occur to you to break out of your circle to feel that the whole world belongs to you, and you to the world?

The self is impatient to pervade the world. It wants to encompass all creation. But we shut it up in a cell. We have made a prisoner of it. We are not conscious of this. From morning till evening we are busy minding the body. Day and night we worry about how fat or thin we are. One would think that there was no other joy in the world. Even beasts experience the pleasures of the senses. Will you not now taste the joy of giving? What joy there is in giving away your full plate of food to a hungry man, though you suffer from hunger! Taste the joy of this experience. A mother, when she works hard for the sake of her child, knows something of this joy. Even when a man draws a small circle around something and calls it 'his own', he does it in pursuit of happiness which he receives for a little while. But what sort of happiness is that? It is like the prisoner coming out of his cell into the courtyard. This is not enough for the spirit. The spirit wants the joy of unbounded freedom.

Philosophy of action

Behind a man's action there are generally two types of attitude. One is the assured feeling, "I shall enjoy the fruit of my action. I have a right to it" and its corollary, "If I am not to enjoy the fruit of my action, then I will not act at all." The other attitude of mind is, "I must of course act; action is complete in itself." The man who acts no doubt has a right to the fruit. But give up this right of your own free will and your action will be truly creative. In other words, do the work, but give up the fruit; and giving up the fruit, do the work. Before, or after, do not hanker after the fruit, but act with full energy and skill. The action of the person who acts without desire should be much better than that of the person who acts with desire. The latter is attracted to the fruit, which means that a part of his time and attention will be spent on thoughts and dreams of the fruit. But the man who has no desire for the fruit devotes all his time and energy to the action. The river takes no rest, the wind knows no fatigue, and the sun can only shine and shine forever. The disinterested doer, too, cannot but render unremitting service. What action then can equal that of the man who thus always rejoices in action? For him action and its result are not separate.

The man of desires looks at an act with the eye of self-interest: "The act is mine, and the fruit too is mine." Because of this, it does not appear to him a moral lapse if his attention strays a little from the work. At most, it seems to him an error in execution. But he who acts without desire for the fruit of his action feels a sense of fulfilment. So with deep and total attention he takes care that there is no shortcoming in his action. For him renunciation of the fruit is the most effective way to right action. And that is *yoga*, the art of living.

Leaving aside the matter of desireless action, there is in the action itself a joy which you cannot find in the fruit. While performing an action for its own sake, one's absorption in it is itself a stream of joy. If you said to an artist, "Don't paint pictures; I shall pay you for not painting," he would not agree. There is a pure joy in the process itself. And this joy itself is the real fruit of action. Weighed against this, the outer, the material fruit is secondary.

Only by taking man's attention away from the fruit can total involvement be created. The disinterested worker's total presence in his work is itself an experience of oneness. His joy is many times greater than that of others. Desireless action is itself a great reward. The tree yields fruit. Would you have the fruit yield further fruit? When this body, like a tree, has brought forth the beautiful fruit of disinterested pursuit of action, why look for any other fruit? Eat action itself, drink action itself, digest action itself. A child plays for the joy of playing. The benefit of exercise comes of its own accord. But the child does not think of this benefit. His joy is in playing. While you act you must not desire freedom from action. Freedom from desire is liberation.

Action without desire is *Karma-yoga*. In *karma-yoga* one surrenders the fruit; but does the fruit come to one, nevertheless? The third chapter of the *Bhagavad Gita* says that the *karma-yogi*, by giving up the fruit of his action, does not lose it, but paradoxically enough gains it in infinite measure.

The ordinary man puts up a fence around his fruit; but by doing so, he loses the infinite fruit that should have been his. The worldly man, after endless toil, receives a small reward; but the *karma-yogi*, though he may do little, receives immense benefit. The difference is only in the inward attitude. Tolstoy says: "People talk a lot about the sacrifice of Jesus Christ; but no one knows how much the worldly man runs about every day of his life and grows dry within! He carries on his back the burden of two donkeys and capers about. Is not his suffering much greater, his plight far worse, than Jesus Christ's?"

Worldly people also labour arduously but in pursuit of low aims. We reap what we sow; as is the desire, so is the fruit. The world will not pay more for our goods than the price we ourselves mark on them. However simple a word may be, the use of it as a *mantra* (charged words) increases its value, its power. What, after all, is a currency note? If we burn it, we might, perhaps, be able to warm a drop of water. The stamp on it gives its value.

This is the whole beauty of *karma-yoga*. Action is like the currency note. Its value is in the feeling behind it, the stamp it bears. There is great beauty in the idea of worshipping an image. This image, in the beginning, was merely a piece of stone. I put life into it. I filled it with my feelings. How can anyone destroy my feelings? Stones can be smashed, but not feelings. When I withdraw my feelings from the image, then what remains will be a mere stone, a thing which anyone can break to pieces.

Action is like a piece of stone, or a piece of paper. My mother scribbled three or four lines on a piece of paper and sent it to me; another gentleman sent me a long discursive fifty-page letter. Now which is more weighty? The feeling in my mother's few lines is beyond measure; it is sacred. The other stuff cannot stand comparison with it. Action must be moistened with love, filled with feelings.

There is a passage in the ancient Indian Law by Manu: A student lived twelve years in his guru's house. He went there an animal, and came out a wise man. What fee was he to give his guru? Fees were not collected in advance. After studying for twelve years one gave the teacher what was proper. Manu says, "Give the Master one or two leaves and flowers, a fan or a pair of sandals, or a water-vessel." Don't think this is a joke; for whatever is to be given should be given with the knowledge that it is a symbol. What, after all, is the worth of a flower? But in the eyes of a devotee, it is equal to all creation.

Suppose two men go for a bathe in the Ganges. One of them says, "What is this Ganges that people talk so much about? Take two parts of hydrogen and one of oxygen; combine the two gases – it becomes Ganges. What else is there in the Ganges?" The other says, "The Ganges flows from the lovely lotus-feet of Lord Vishnu. She has dwelt in the matted hair of Shiva. Thousands of seers, both ascetic and kingly, have done penance near her. Countless holy acts have been performed by her side. Such is the sacred Ganges, my mother." Filled with this feeling, he bathes in the river. The other man, regarding it as combination of hydrogen and oxygen, also bathes. Both derive the benefit of physical cleansing. But the devotee gets the benefit of mental purification as well. Even a buffalo, if it bathes in the Ganges, will achieve physical cleanliness. The dirt of the body will go. But how to wash the mind of its taint? One got the petty benefit of physical cleanliness; the other, in addition, gained the invaluable fruit of inward purity.

The action is the same; but a distinction arises from the difference in the inward attitude. The action of the man who seeks spiritual good promotes the growth of the soul; the action of the worldly man serves to bind it. If the karma-yogi is a farmer, he will till the land, considering it his svadharma. His stomach will, of course, be filled; but he does not work to fill his stomach. He looks upon food as a means by which he keeps his body fit for the task of tilling the land. The end is svadharma and food is the means. But to the farmer who is not a *karma-yogi*, filling his stomach is the end, and his *svadharma*, farming, is the means. The two attitudes are thus the reverse of each other.

When others are awake, the *karma-yogi* is asleep; and when others are asleep, the *karma-yogi* is awake. Just as we take good care to keep the stomach filled, the *karma-yogi* is watchful lest even one moment should slip past without action. If he too eats, it is out of necessity. The night of the one is the day of the other; and the day of the one is the night of the other. Though the actions of the worldly man and the *karma-yogi* look alike, the *karma-yogi's* distinction is that he has given up attachment to the fruit of his action, and finds joy in the action itself.

By desireless action both the individual and society are richly blessed. Because he is always absorbed in right action, his body keeps healthy and the society in which he lives prospers. For example, the *karma-yogi* farmer will not cultivate opium or tobacco which would bring him a high profit. Action done as *svadharma* confers nothing but benefit on the community. The *karma-yogi* lives without ego and he is one with the community around him.

Through action the *karma-yogi* attains a state of being which is pure. His action is a form of prayer. His mind is purified by it, and the clear mind receives true knowledge. As the *karma-yogi* barber washed people's hair, wisdom came to him. "Look, I remove the dirt from others' heads, but have I ever removed the dirt from my own head, from my own mind?" The language of the spirit came to him through his work. As he weeds his field, the *karma-yogi* farmer gets the idea of removing the weeds of passion from his own heart. As the yogi potter kneads and moulds the raw clay and gives baked pots to the people, he learns the lesson that his own life is a pot that needs to be baked and moulded. He can test with his fingers if a pot is baked or raw; he thus becomes a judge of saintliness. From this it is evident that the *karma-yogi*, through the terms of his own trade or occupation, gains knowledge of perfection. What was their trade but a school of the spirit? These actions of theirs were nothing but worship, nothing but service. Viewed from without, these actions looked worldly, but in reality, they were spiritual. The *karma-yogi* may reach the summit of spiritual liberation. In spite of this achievement he does not give up his everyday activity.

If the yogi were to sit in silence, others too would follow his example and sit with folded hands. The yogi, ever content, loses himself in inner happiness, and remains quiet; but others, inwardly weeping, become inactive. One is at rest because he is happy at heart; the other is merely passive. This state is terrifying. It encourages vanity and hypocrisy. That is why all the yogis, even after reaching the heights, have, with good reason, held on to the apron-strings of action, have kept on performing their *karma* till death. The mother delights in her children's games with their dolls. Though she knows that it is only make-believe, she joins in and creates in the children's interest in the game. If she takes no part, the children find no fun in it. If the *karma-yogi* gives up action, others, even though they have the need for it, may follow his example and, in giving up action remain spiritually hungry and joyless. The *karma-yogi* does not think that he is in any way an exceptional person. He exerts himself infinitely more than other men. It is not necessary to put a stamp on any action and mark it as spiritual. There is no need to advertise one's action. If you are a perfect seeker of the real, then let your actions show a hundred times more zest than other men's.

We have developed some absurd ideas about the spirit. People imagine that once a man has become spiritual, there is no more need for him to move hand or foot, or do any work. They say, "What sort of religious man is this, who ploughs the fields and weaves?" But nobody asks how a spiritual man can eat food. The God of the *karma-yoga*, Krishna, brushes down horses, clears the leaf-plates after the feast, and goes out into the forest to graze cows, playing on his flute. So the yogis have pictured Krishna as God of action and they themselves have done the work of tailor, potter, weaver, gardener, trader, barber or cobbler. Doing these things, they have found themselves and become free.

The actions reveal the real quality of our minds. The surface of the water is clear; but throw a stone into it, and at once the mud rises up. At the bottom of the still lake there is knee-deep mud. It is only when an object from without touches it that one can see it. We say "Anger has come to a man." Did that anger come from without? No, it was within – else it could never have shown itself.

People say that they prefer coloured dresses to white, because "coloured doesn't get dirty". That, too, gets dirty, but the dirt does not show. Our action is like the white cloth. It proclaims that we are given to anger, or selfishness, or something else. Action is the mirror which shows us our true form. Would we smash a mirror because it shows us a dirty, ugly face? On the contrary, we should thank it and go and wash our face. Similarly, if, through action, the defects and weaknesses of our mind are revealed, should we then wish to avoid action? Will our minds become pure by our turning away from action?

A man goes and sits in a cave, cut off from all human contact. He imagines that he has attained perfect calm of mind. But let him leave the cave and go out to beg for his food. A mischievous little boy rattles the bolt of a door, and is absorbed in contemplating the noise it makes, but the yogi cannot bear the music that the innocent child enjoys. By living in a cave he has made his mind so weak that he cannot stand the slightest jolt. A little rattling noise shatters his peace of mind.

When defects come to light we can get rid of them. If they are hidden from sight, progress is obstructed and growth comes to an end. When we act and discover our own defects then we learn how to remain unattached.

Desirelessness is a state of mind. As a means of creating this, the pursuit of *svadharma* is not enough; other aids are needed. To light a lamp one needs not only the oil and the wick, but a flame. When the lamp is lit, the darkness disappears. How is this lamp to be lit? To light it we need to purify the mind which can be done by self-examination.

As long as the mind is not as pure and peaceful as a mountain stream desirelessness will not come to us. These actions performed to purify the mind are called *'vikarma'*. The three words, *'karma'*, *'vikarma'* and *'akarma'*, from the *Gita*, are of the utmost importance. *Karma* is the concrete, outward action performed as *svadharma*. The participation of the pure mind and heart in this external action is *'vikarma'*. We bow our heads to someone, but if, while we are doing this, the heart too does not bow, the external act is meaningless. The inner and outer must become one. The action and the actor must become inseparable.

When *vikarma*, the action of the mind and heart, enters into *karma*, desirelessness grows within us, little by little. As the body and the mind are separate, each has its own means of growth. When they are in harmony the goal is within our reach. Lest the body and the mind should go different ways, we take the path of austerity without and meditation within. When the mind does not meditate, outer forms of austerity, like fasting, are entirely wasted. While doing penance the inward flame should constantly burn. If we give up the pleasures of the senses and are not united with the inward flame, of what value is the physical act of fasting? If, instead of thinking of God, we think of things to eat and drink, the fast becomes more dangerous than a feast! There is nothing as terrible as this mental feasting, as thinking about pleasures. *Tantra* must be accompanied by *mantra*, action by meditation. Action as such has no value, nor mere meditation without action.

If the outward action is not moistened by the heart's affection, then the performance of *svadharma* is barren, it does not bear the flower and the fruit of desirelessness. Suppose we are nursing a sick man only out of a sense of duty and without compassion, it becomes dull and disgusting to us, and a burden instead of a relief to the patient. Moreover, where the heart is not engaged, egoism shows its head. We entertain expectations like this: "I served him today. He should serve me at my need; he should admire and praise me." Or else we get fed up and say, "I do so much for him, and yet he keeps complaining." Sick men are usually peevish – and those who nurse them without the right spirit will only be disgusted.

When the inner flame illuminates the action, the latter is transformed. When the flame is applied to the wick in the oil, light is born. When *vikarma* is applied to *karma*, desirelessness comes into being. When a spark touches the gunpowder, it explodes. In the same way, the infinite power of the practice of *svadharma* is latent. Touch it with *vikarma*, and see what work it can do! In the resulting explosion desire and anger are destroyed, and a power is released which results in *akarma* (inaction in action). This means that, while acting, we seem not to act, we do not feel the burden of action. Though we act, we are not the doer. By *vikarma*, by inner purity, *karma* ceases to be *karma*. An action performed with pure heart does not attach itself to us. It leaves no residue of sin or virtue. The problem of morality, the goodness and badness of action, distracts us. We feel that action crowds in on us from all sides, we feel that it has caught us by the throat. Just as the waves of the sea dash with force against the land and make channels into it, the complexity of action *(karma)* enters the mind and agitates it. The quality of pleasure and pain develops; all peace is lost. The action takes place, and is over, but its force remains behind. Action corrupts the mind, and destroys sleep.

But if with *karma* we combine *vikarma*, then, however much work we do, we will not feel its strain. The mind becomes still, steady and radiant.

How does *karma* become *akarma* – how does action become inactivity, and inactivity become action? To see it fully, we have to sit at the feet of a yogi. He, though engaged in a thousand actions, does not allow a ripple to arise in the still waters of his mind. We can learn this from him, it cannot be learned from books, although nowadays books have become very cheap and they are in plenty. Education too is widely

spread and costs little. Universities seem to distribute knowledge in neat little packets. But no one seems to be satisfied
with feeding on this nectar of knowledge. The more one looks
at this mountain of books, the more one realises how necessary it is to serve the yogis. Behind these book-heaps, the King
of Knowledge sits hidden.

Gita says: You have been listening to so many things that
your mind is dazed. Till it becomes empty and steady, you will
not see the way clearly. Stop reading books and listening to
people and take sanctuary with the yogis. There you can read
the book of life. There, silent speech clears all your doubts. By
going to them you will understand how utterly serene the
mind can be while performing continuous action – and not
being indulgent in *samsara* (worldly attachment), which has
been compared to an ocean. In the ocean, wherever you look,
you see nothing but water; *samsara* too, is like that. It surrounds you on all sides. If you give up home and go to the
forest, there too you find that the same *samsara* occupies the
mind. If you go and sit in a cave, the loin-cloth embodies *samsara*. The loin-cloth becomes for you the essence of all possessiveness. Because you renounce your family, narrow your circle, *samsara* has not therefore relaxed its hold on you; by reducing your possessions, you do not reduce your possessiveness.
Whether you say ten twenty-fifths or two-fifths it means the
same. Whether at home or in the forest, attachment is ever
with us. The pressure of *samsara* is no lighter.

The universe of *samsara* pursues us in such a way that, even
when we live within the bounds of *svadharma*, it never lets us
go. Though you have given up all distracting activities and
complications, and have retained *samsara* in name only, you
still remain possessive. *Samsara*, like a demon, can assume a
larger or smaller form. Big or small, a demon is a demon. What
is inescapable is the same wherever you are, in a palace or in a
hut. Reducing the area of your activity is not the same as being
unattached to and getting beyond craving and anger, greed
and delusion. If we endeavour constantly to keep action free

of impurity, then, later, pure *karma* will go on of itself. When once actions do not distort the mind, but take place naturally, one after the other, we do not notice that they have taken place at all.

When a child first learns to walk how much effort he puts into it! But later, walking becomes natural. He walks and he talks. He does not think about it. Our ideal is to perform the *karma* in accordance with our *svadharma*. The mind will reach a stage where it will not feel the slightest effort in action. Though thousands of actions are done by our hands, the mind remains clear and calm. If you look up and question the sky, "Brother sky, do you not get scorched by the sun, and wet with the rain? Don't you shiver with the cold?", what answer do you expect? Will it not say, "You can settle what happens to me; I know nothing."

"Whether the man who is man is naked or clad.
  Is a matter which bothers only the others."

This means that when we go on performing actions which are our *svadharma*, these actions become natural to us. Even the most trying situations do not seem difficult. This is the key to *karma-yoga*. If we try to force open a lock without a key, we will only bruise our hands; with the key we can open it in no time. This master-key, which eliminates all strain and trouble, we get by conquering the mind. In other words, we should wash off the dirt that appears in the mind in the course of action. Then outward action will cease to cause trouble; even the feeling that "I am the doer" will vanish; actor and the action will become one; craving and anger will lose their power; there will be no trace of effort. Even the awareness of action will not remain.

The mother tends the child. Does she ever want to publish reports on it? If she cared for publicity, we could say, "Thank you" and discharge our debt to her. But she protests,"What have I done? I've done nothing. Is this a burden to me?"

When the sun rises, does it enter its mind to say, "I shall banish the darkness, I shall urge the birds to fly, and set men working"? The sun stands still, where it rises. But the very fact of its being makes all the world go round. The sun is not aware of this. If you said to the sun, "O Sun-God, the help you give is infinite, how much darkness you have dispelled!"it would make no sense to him. He says, "Bring a little darkness and show it to me. If I can dispel it, I shall accept that I am the doer." How can one carry darkness to the sun? Because the sun exists, darkness is dispelled. In the light of the sun one man may read a good book and another, an obscene one; one may set fire to his neighbour's house, another help a neighbour. But the sun is not responsible for the good or the evil of these acts. The sun says, "Light is my nature. What else but light could there be in me? I am not aware that I am shedding light. For me, to be is to shine. I am not aware of the strain of giving light. I do not feel that I am doing anything."

'Being' is the basis of *akarma*. The actions become so much a part of one's being and nature that one is not conscious of their happening. Actions become worship, and speech moves to virtue, for *karma* has become *akarma*. Every morning the cock crows; this is its natural function. But no one ever thinks of giving the cock a speech of thanks and appreciation. We expect no recognition for acting according to our nature. It is only natural for a yogi to do things like telling the truth, loving all creatures, finding no fault in others, and being of service to everyone. They cannot live otherwise. Do we specially honour a man for eating? Service to others comes naturally to a yogi, just as eating, drinking and sleeping do to ordinary people. It is impossible for him to say, "I shall not help". We should take it that the *karma* of such a yogi has become *akarma*.

What is the state of *sannyasa*? It is giving up all action. To be free from all action, not to act at all, that is *sannyasa*. But what does 'not acting' mean? Action is a curious thing. How can we give up all action? Action is in front of us and behind us, to right and left of us; it spreads all round us in every direction. Why, if we sit down, that too is action. When doing nothing itself turns out to be an action, how is it possible to give up action? And how are we to avoid action which goes on even when we are doing nothing? There is a way of renouncing action, and that is to devise a method by which, though we do all the actions in the world, they melt and flow away from us. Then the state of *sannyasa* is reached.

One aspect of this state of *akarma* is that, though the man acts, he does not act. The other aspect is that, though he does not act at all, he moves the whole world to action. There is in him an immeasurable power to impel to action. This is the paradox of *akarma;* it is filled with a power that is capable of infinite action. It is like steam which, when compressed, does enormous work. Steam that is enclosed gains tremendous power, and moves huge ships and long trains. It is the same with the sun which does nothing at all but works twenty-four hours in the day. If asked, the sun would say, "I do nothing at all." One aspect of the sun is that it works day and night and yet does nothing; the other, that while it does nothing, it performs infinite action day and night.

In respect of one, the action is explicit, and the state of *akarma* is filled to overflowing with action, and thus mighty actions are achieved. There is a world of difference between the man in this state, and the idler. The lazy man gets easily tired and depressed. But the *sannyasi*, who does no work, conserves his power. He does not work at all. That is, he does not work with his limbs, or with his mind. But even while he does nothing, he does infinite work.

Supposing someone we have offended does not speak to us when we go to him. How great is the effect of his silence, his 'renunciation of speech'! Another man in the same situation splutters out his indignation. Both are angry, but while one does not open his mouth, the other bursts out. Both are examples of anger. How terrible it is for a child when its mother stops speaking to it! Not speaking, giving up action, is far more effective than any kind of positive action. Silence can achieve what speaking cannot. Such is the state of the yogi. His non-action, his silence, his sitting still, accomplishes much, releases great power for action. In such *sannyasa* all initiative and all effort come together and rest in one place.

> The movement of action has stopped.
> All care is over, and faith has come;
> I dwell no more in the womb.
> Not in my own being do I live;
> I live in the being of the One.
> I am empty and hollow.

This idea of *sannyasa*, one may say, is the highest point reached by man's intellect, his power of thought. Beyond this no man's thought has stretched. There is a rare joy in the very contemplation of this *sannyasa* with its two aspects. On this matter, I have thought and talked with my friends for many years, and I have discovered the inadequacy of language to deal with it.

Between action and activity there is a difference. For example, there is a big commotion somewhere, and we want to stop it. A policeman shouts at the top of his voice to put an end to the noise. He had to perform the intense action of shouting aloud. Another person comes up and merely lifts his finger. With only this the people become quiet. A third person has but to come there and stillness descends. One had to exert himself and perform an action; the action of the second was a gentle gesture; the action of the third was subtle. Activity becomes progressively less; but all three alike do the work of calming the people. As inward purity grows, the effort in the action becomes less. From effort to gentleness, from gentleness to subtlety, and from subtlety to nothingness. When the mind and heart become absolutely pure, activity tends towards zero and action towards infinity.

In this last state, the yogi becomes ego-less. He loses attachment to the body, reaches the end of activity and attains a new state of being which is not a state of activity. It is a delightful concept of doing everything by doing nothing, and doing nothing in doing everything. Is the *karma-yogi* (he who does nothing while doing everything) better, or the *karma-sannyasi* (he who does everything while doing nothing)? Who really does more work? It is impossible to answer these questions. Doing nothing through doing all things, to do all things by doing nothing – both alike are *yoga;* but for the sake of comparison, one is called *yoga*, the other *sannyasa.*

Both the *sannyasi* and the *karma-yogi* are seers, and are entitled to the same high throne. Though the names are different, the substance is the same. They are two modes of the same reality. A wheel in rapid motion seems at rest. The state of the *sannyasi* is similar. From his peace and steadiness flows infinite power, endless movement.

Though this is true, yet the *karma-yoga* is better than *sannyasa* from the standpoint of the seeker after perfection. To do nothing, and yet to do all things is possible for the perfected one, not for the seeker. But he can practise in some measure the method of doing all things and yet doing nothing. Action through inaction is a riddle beyond the understanding of the seeker. *Karma-yoga* is both the way and the goal, but *sannyasa* is only the goal.

Many people mistakenly imagine that the spiritual life is intended only for ascetics. When a man says "I am not an ascetic" he seems to imply that ascetics are a species, like horses, lions, bears and cows; and that the spiritual life is only intended for that species. It is as if all other creatures in the work-a-day world belong to some different species with thoughts and ways of its own. Such thinking has divided humanity into two kinds of being, ascetics and worldly men. But the truth is that spiritual understanding is for every man and for ordinary men, living their daily lives in the world. The higher knowledge teaches us how, by keeping our lives pure through *karma*, the action, we can attain equilibrium and peace of mind. Therefore, don't raise a fence round yourself, saying, "I am an ordinary fellow, wallowing in worldliness. What can I do? My whole being is contained in this six-foot body." Let a man raise the self by the Self; let him not debase himself.

Through meditation everyone can raise himself to a state of a yogi. There are three important things in the way of meditation, namely (1) one-pointedness of mind, (2) setting bounds to one's life, and (3) a state of equanimity or evenness of vision. One-pointedness of mind means controlling its movements. Setting bounds to one's life means doing actions after weighing and understanding them. Evenness of vision means having the ability to think in terms of the whole, the total, the complete. These three together make up meditation.

To make the mind perfectly calm is a great thing. Unless you stop the revolving wheel of thoughts, how can you attain one-pointedness? Even if the outer wheel is somehow stopped, the inner wheel will go on revolving. As we use more and more external means to concentrate the mind, the inner wheels revolve all the faster. You may cross your legs, sit straight, and fix your gaze. But the mind won't become one-pointed because of this. The important thing is to be able to still the wheels of the mind and have a balanced outlook. Without this, the mind cannot become one-pointed. The lion is the mighty king of the forest and yet he does not take four steps forward without looking behind. How can the lion, that lives by violence, attain concentration of mind? The eyes of the lion, the crow and the cat constantly rove about. Their look shows fear and suspicion. Such is the state of animals that are violent. But we should develop a sense of equanimity. All creation should appear to us auspicious and friendly. I should trust all creatures as I trust myself. What have we to fear? All things are pure, all things holy. This universe is auspicious. Nothing is wrong with this universe. If there is anything wrong, it is my vision. As is my vision, so is the world. If I wear red glasses, the world appears red and aflame. "Beauty is in the eye of the beholder." For as long as we do not feel sure that the whole creation is auspicious, the mind will not be one-pointed. As long as we think that something is wrong with the universe, we look at all things with suspicion. Those whose minds are filled with the fear, what can they know of peace and one-pointedness? Once you start seeing friendliness everywhere, the mind will, of itself, attain peace.

When I am tired I go to the banks of a clear running river. At the sight of the pure, calm, flowing water I cease to be restless. I forget all troubles. How did this moving water gain such power? The stream flows without a break, it has no resting-place, no home of its own, but this pure stream calms my mind in a moment. When I look at such a lovely stream, does not a spring of love and wisdom well up in my heart? If this lifeless water can confer such serenity on my mind, how much deeper the peace if, in the valley of the mind, there should spring up the living stream of wisdom.

On the same kind of paper and with the same brush, an artist paints a variety of pictures. The *vina*-player, out of seven notes, makes so many different *ragas* (modes of music). With the few letters in the alphabet we express endless variety of thought and feeling. Look on this creation too in the same light. There are in it innumerable objects, and many modes of being. But all this exterior and interior creation is made up of two things – the indivisible *atman* (the Self) and the eight-fold forms of *prakriti* (Nature). The anger of the angry man, the love of the lover, the agony of the sufferer, the happiness of the happy one, the drowsiness of the idler, the activity of the worker – all these are the play of the same power of consciousness. At the root of all these contradictory movements, and feeding them all, is a single Consciousness. As the Consciousness within is one, so too is the outer veil single in its nature. All creation is born of *atman*, the self, and *prakriti*, the Nature.

While everywhere spirit and body, the supernatural and the natural, are thus one, why is man caught in illusion? Why does he differentiate? While the face of a loving man is pleasant to look at, the sight of another fills us with disgust. Why are we attracted by one and repelled by the other?

This man is near to me, the other distant; this is mine, that is his – such thoughts arise in our minds, and on occasion deflect us from our duty all because of delusion. If we are to escape this, we should learn the secret of the creative skill of the Lord's fingers. The same drum gives out many kinds of sound. Some frighten us, others make us dance. If we are to master all these emotions, we have to catch hold of the drummer. Once he is in our hands, all the notes too are in our hands. Lord Krishna says: "Those who wish to cross *maya*, the dream, let them take refuge in me. Only those who are surrendered to me will escape the play of *maya*; for them, the waters of *maya* dry up here and now."

What is this that we call *maya*? The power of God. His art, the skill of His hand – His divine drama – this is what we call *maya*. *Maya* is nothing but the power of the Creator who, out of *atman* (the consciousness) and *prakriti* (the Nature) creates an endless variety of things. Seeing this, we experience many contradictory emotions of good and bad. If we, transcending these, wish to attain true peace, we should try and catch hold of the maker of them all. It is only when we come to know Him that we can escape the delusion which causes division and attachment.

The yogis worship the serpent, the elephant-headed God, and trees. From the ant to the sun and the moon, in all that they see, they behold the Lord, and in their hearts are the waves of the ocean of joy. An endless bliss. This divine vision, you may call an illusion if you like. In the majestic ocean they see the grandeur of the Lord; in Mother Cow, the mother-like tenderness of God; in the earth, His patience; in the clear sky, His purity; in sun, moon and stars, His brightness and beauty. In the flower they see His softness, and in evil men, the Lord who tests and tries us. Thus they practise the art of seeing the one God at play everywhere, and doing so, one day, the yogi merges into the Lord.

Does the Lord hide Himself somewhere, in some cave or crevice, in some river or in some heaven? Diamonds and rubies, gold and silver, lie hidden in the bowels of the earth, pearls and corals in the depths of the sea. But is this gem, the Lord, hidden somewhere? Have we to dig Him up? No, He stands all the time before all of us. Everyone is a manifestation of the Lord. Do not dishonour the person of the Lord manifest in human form. It is the Lord that appears as all things moving and unmoving. Where is the need for artificial aids to seek and find Him? The way is straight and easy. Relate to the Lord whatever action you perform.

The most charming part of Lord Krishna's life is his childhood. It is the young Krishna that we cherish in our hearts and worship. He goes out with other cowherd boys grazing cattle; he eats and laughs and plays with them. When they set out to worship God, he told them, "Who has seen God? How has he helped us? But this *Govardhan* hill stands here before our eyes. Our cattle graze on its slopes. Streams flow from it. Let us therefore worship it." Such things he taught them. To his cowherd companions, to the *gopis* (the young girls), with whom he laughed and talked, to the cows and calves he rejoiced in, to them all he opened the door of liberation. He moved with cows and calves in his childhood, with horses when he grew up. On hearing the music of his flute the cows went into ecstasy; the horses thrilled to the touch of his hand as he stroked them. The cows and calves, the chariot-horses, were filled with Krishna, became one with Him. Lord Krishna made it clear that not only men but animals and birds also had the right to *moksha*, the ultimate liberation.

Moksha does not depend on one's learning of or performance of rites. All it needs is straight and simple life with dedication. While learned men who say, "I, I," are left behind, innocent and devout ones go forward. When the mind is pure and the heart full of simplicity, *moksha* is not difficult to attain. The learned King Janaka approaches a woman to learn wisdom from her. We see Sulabha (the innocent), teaching divine wisdom to King Janaka. She is an ordinary woman, and he an emperor, and a profound scholar. But the wise Janaka had not attained *moksha*.

Karma-yoga and *bhakti-yoga* have to be beautifully blended. It is like planting a walnut tree. The walnut tree takes twenty-five years to yield fruit. The man who plants it rarely gets the chance of eating in his own lifetime the fruit of the tree he planted. And yet he has to plant and water and look after the tree lovingly. *Karma-yoga* means planting and minding the tree but not desiring the fruit, and *bhakti-yoga,* means becoming one with the Lord by dedicating everything to him.

Let us act and not throw away the fruit but dedicate it to God. To throw away the fruit would be to reject it, but dedication is different. When *karma* and *bhakti* are combined in one then it is *raja-yoga.* "The benefit of your *karma* goes to someone, doesn't it? If so, give it over to the Lord, dedicate it to Him." *Raja-yoga* points out the proper recipient. There is no negative action of renouncing the fruit in *raja-yoga:* everything is dedicated to the Lord. The gift that is offered to the Lord is always pure. Even if there are impurities in your action, it will become pure when it reaches His hands. However hard we try to make our actions perfect there will still be some shortcomings. Nevertheless, let us act with the utmost possible purity. Why only the fruit, even the deformations like lust and anger – place them all at the feet of the Lord, and be free from care. Here there is no need to torture oneself in the fire of self-guilt. Surrender promptly and find freedom. No holding down or cutting off.

We need not go and sit in a cave to worship God. Whatever action we perform, wherever we may perform it, surrender it to God. The mother waiting on her child waits on God. When she bathes her child, she is performing an act for God. The mother, regarding the child as a gift from God, should tend it with devotion. The mother's act of tender care is indeed noble. What greater fortune could come to her than serving the image of the Lord, her child? When we serve each other, if only we did it with this attitude, how transformed our actions would be! We should have the feeling that whatever work comes to us is the service of the Lord Himself.

The moments of our daily life may appear commonplace, but in reality they are not so; they carry enormous signifi-

cance. All one's life is a great *karma*, a continual sacrificial performance. What is sleep? It is an experience of oneness. If we
surrender all our enjoyments to the Lord before we fall asleep,
what is sleep but to transcend? There is a custom among the
Hindus of reciting the hymns of cosmic man while taking a
bath. What is the connection between the Cosmic Person,
with his thousand hands and thousand eyes and this bath?
The connection is that, in the pitcher of water that you pour on
your head, there are thousands of drops. Those drops wash
your head – they rid you of your uncleanliness. It is like the
blessing of the Lord showered on your head. The thousand
hands of the Lord are pouring a thousand drops on your head
and purifying your body, mind and heart. If you pour this
divinity into this act, the bath will assume a new quality and
acquire a boundless power.

Who is to decide that a man is bad? Even if a really bad person appears before you, treat him as if he is the Lord Himself.
Even the villain will become a saint. Who can be certain that
the man is wicked? Once there was a man who, feeling that
there was something inauspicious about his house, left it and
went and settled in another village. That in turn seemed dirty
to him, and he went away to the forest. There, as he sat under
a mango tree, a bird's droppings fell on his head. He said,
"This forest, too, is unfriendly," and went and stood in a river.
In the river the sight of the big fish eating up the small fish filled him with disgust. "The whole of creation," he concluded,
"is unkind. There is no way out except through death". So he
came out of the water and kindled a fire. Then a man who was
passing by said, "My brother, why are you preparing to die?"
He replied, "Because the whole world is inauspicious." The
man said, "If this unclean body of yours, this mass of flesh,
begins to burn, how it will stink! I live close by. Where can I
go? When a single hair burns, it smells so awful! And now, all
this flesh of yours will burn! Just think a little of the stench you
will spread." Then the man was bewildered and exclaimed,
"If one can neither live in this world nor die in it, what is one

109

to do?"

That is to say, if we go about condemning everything as bad and inauspicious, and rejecting it, we simply cannot carry on. In truth, the world, as it is, is auspicious. Where is the need to gather up into a little spot this world of Time and Space? Familiarity breeds contempt. We should be intimate with some things and keep others at a distance. Before our teacher we sit humbly, at a distance. But with our mother we go and sit in her lap. There is an appropriate way of dealing with the various images of reality. While we draw close to a flower, we step back from the fire. The beauty of the stars is in their distance. This is so with all creation. It is not as if we shall increase our joy by bringing very near to us that which is very far away. Real pleasure lies in letting things be wherever they are. We cannot say that something that gives delight from afar will always confer greater comfort when brought near. We should leave it, out there, and enjoy it from afar. There is no meaning in an enforced familiarity. Man is drawn by distant objects. Distance has an attraction. What is by his side lies neglected in a corner and he has dreams of what is far away. But this is an illusion. Though the *svadharma* that is mine seems commonplace, incomplete and uninteresting, yet because it is mine, it is the best for me; it is the most beautiful to me. When a man is drowning in the sea it is the log floating near him, however rough and gnarled, that will save him. Does it matter that it is not well-shaped, smooth and polished? In the carpenter's shed there may be any number of beautiful, well-hewn pieces of wood. But they are in the workshop, while he is struggling for life in the sea. This rough, unshapely log alone can save him. He must catch hold of it.

But how are we to overcome the danger of egoism? That is possible through steadfast wisdom within us. We should make *sattva* (purity) not a guest who comes and goes, but a member of the household. We get proud of things that we do once in a while. We sleep daily, but we do not discuss it with others. If a patient has no sleep at all for a fortnight and then sleeps for a while, he tells everybody, "I had some sleep yesterday." It seems to him quite an event.

When some good action gets done through our hands, we are inclined to take the credit for it and feel proud. Why? Because it was not done naturally. When in the thick darkness of the night there are a few glow-worms, look how proudly they show themselves off! They do not display all their brightness at once. The glow-worm twinkles and stops and twinkles again, as if it were playing hide and seek with light. But if its light were steady, it would not be so proud. Because it is constant, one notices nothing special in it. If, in the same way, purity shines constantly in all our actions, it becomes our nature. Not only is the lion not proud of its strength, it is not even conscious of it. So too, pure conduct must be so natural and spontaneous with us that we do not even think of it.

At our birth we are born into three orders. The first is the universe, the boundless creation. The second is our society. And the third is our body. Every day we use these three orders, we wear them out. In order to replenish what is lost through us we should perform three sets of actions – *yajna*, *dana* and *tapas*, sacrifice, the giving of gifts and austerity.

What is 'yajna'? Every day we make use of Nature. If a hundred of us crowd together in one spot for a day, that part of Nature appears spoiled. We foul the atmosphere and mess up the whole place. In eating food, wearing clothes, etc. we consume the earth's resources. We should make up for this depletion and replace what has been consumed. To make good the loss: that is one purpose of *yajna*. Another purpose is to purify the things we use. We use the well and make the place all round it dirty and slushy. This part of creation is thus disfigured. *Yajna* involves purification of the place. In addition some new construction is included in *yajna*. If we wear clothes, we should spin a little every day and make something new. Growing cotton, raising crops, spinning and weaving, all these are acts of *yajna*, sacrifice. Whatever we do in *yajna* should not be done for our own sake but with the feeling that

111

it is important to make up for the loss that one has caused. This is not altruism. Therefore, by replenishing loss, purifying things and creating new things we discharge our debt to the natural creation which is the first order of our existence.

The second order is our human society – father, mother, teacher, friend and other human beings. 'Dana' (giving) is instituted to discharge our debt to society. I have received from society boundless service. When I came into this world I was weak and helpless. This society brought me up so that I have developed. Therefore I, in my turn, should serve society. The service that we render to free ourselves from our debt to society is *dana*.

The third order, is the body. This too wears out day by day. We wear it out by use of our mind, our knowledge, our senses. 'Tapas' (austerity) has been prescribed in order to remove the defects and distortions that arise in the body.

Thus the right action is to ensure that these three orders – Nature, society and the body – may proceed smoothly and efficiently. We create any number of good and bad institutions; but these three orders are not man-made. They have come to us naturally. Therefore it is our natural *dharma* to replenish through *yajna, dana* and *tapas* the wear and tear in these three orders. We shall need all our energy to keep these three orders – Nature, society and the body – in good condition.

Through *yajna* we maintain equilibrium with Nature, through *dana* in society, and through *tapas* in the body. Thus this programme is intended to preserve the state of balance in all the three orders.

The service that is being rendered to the world through external actions of *yajna, dana* and *tapas*, can be described as spiritual exercise. The service to creation and the development of the spirit do not demand two different courses of action: they are not separate.

When the sculptor gets absorbed in carving, he feels that this beautiful image was not shaped by his hands alone. As he goes on chiselling somehow, from somewhere, beauty emerges. The beauty, the loveliness of the image, is nothing but the beauty of the sculptor's soul that has been poured into it.

Here we have regarded *yajna, dana* and *tapas* as if they were three different things, but there is no difference between them. For the three orders of Nature, society and the body are not absolutely distinct. Society is not outside creation; nor for that matter is the body. These three together make up the order of Nature. The creative effort we make, the *dana* we give and the *tapas* we perform, all these can be called *yajna* in the comprehensive sense.

In all these actions *mantra*, too, is necessary. (*Mantra* is a word which relates action to the feeling behind it.) Action without *mantra* is meaningless. If we work for hours on end, but without *mantra* in our heart, it is all wasted. The mind will not attain purity through mere work. Take spinning for example. If we apply to the action this *mantra* that the Lord hidden in the cotton manifests Himself in the form of the thread, the action will become truly pure. It will become worship, service, to the people and to God. In this thread charged with *mantra*, you will begin to see the whole universe.

There will be no conflict in a society where *yajna, dana* and *tapas* are found, where actions take place accompanied by *mantra*, contemplation. As, when two mirrors face each other, each is reflected in the other, in the same way, true to the laws of reflection, the individual and society will mutually strengthen peace. My happiness is that of society, and society's is mine. We can examine each of these and find that they are both one. We shall experience *advaita*, oneness, everywhere. Separateness shall disappear.